A LESSON FOR EVERY DAY

9-10 YEARS

LITERACY

9-10 YEARS

WITHDRAWN

Published 2010 by A & C Black Publishers Limited
36 Soho Square, London W1D 3QY
www.acblack.com

ISBN 978-1-4081-2541-0

Copyright text © Christine Moorcroft 2010
Editors: Dodi Beardshaw, Jane Klima, Marie Lister, Clare Robertson, Lynne Williamson
Compiled by Mary Nathan and Fakenham Photosetting

The authors and publishers would like to thank Ray Barker, Fleur Lawrence and Rifat Siddiqui for their advice in producing this series of books.

The author and publishers are grateful for permission to reproduce the following:
p.33 Extracts from Bill's New Frock and How to Write Really Badly by Anne Fine (Egmont UK), reproduced by permission of David Higham Associates on behalf of Anne Fine; p.37 Extract from The Water Horse by Dick King-Smith, (Viking 1990, Puffin 1992), © Fox Busters Limited 1990, reproduced by permission of Penguin Books Ltd; p.38 Extract from The Sheep Pig by Dick King-Smith (Victor Gollancz/Hamish Hamilton 1983) © Dick King-Smith, 1983, reproduced by permission of Penguin Books Ltd; p.91 'Cinderella' from Revolting Rhymes by Roald Dahl (Jonathan Cape Ltd & Penguin Books Ltd), reproduced with permission of David Higham Associates on behalf of the Roald Dahl Estate; p.193 'Taking my pen for a walk' reproduced by kind permission of the author, Julie O'Callaghan; p.209 'The Listeners' by Walter de la Mare, reproduced by permission of the Literary Trustees of Walter de la Mare and The Society of Authors as their representative; p.213 'Leisure' by W H Davies, reproduced by permission of Kieron Griffin as Trustee of the Mrs H M Davies Will. Every effort has been made to trace copyright holders and obtain their permission for use of copyright material. The publishers would be pleased to rectify any error or omission in future editions.

A CIP catalogue record for this book is available from the British Library.

Printed and bound in Great Britain by Martins the Printers, Berwick-on-Tweed.

A & C Black uses paper produced with elemental chlorine-free pulp, harvested from managed sustainable forests.

A Martian comes to stay Stories by Penelope Lively **7. Understanding and interpreting texts** Explore how writers use language for comic and dramatic effects	**A Martian comes to stay** and **Stories by Penelope Lively** provide an opportunity to introduce an author through a short story and to encourage the children to read her other work. The children might see the humour in the matter-of-fact response of Peter and his gran to a Martian knocking at the front door and in the everyday language Gran uses to talk about him: 'Should have offered him a cup of tea. He'll have had a fair journey.' You could draw out that, unlike in some children's stories (for example, *Come Away From the Water Shirley* by John Burningham and *Andrew's Bath* by David McPhail) the adult believes the improbable-sounding messages from the child rather than just humouring him or her. Draw the children's attention to the real-life setting and the relationship between the realistic characters in this setting and a fantastical character. This then can be found in other stories by Penelope Lively: for instance *The Ghost of Thomas Kempe*.	**Reading AF2** Understand, describe, select or retrieve information, events or ideas from texts and use quotation and reference to text **Reading AF3** Deduce, infer or interpret information, events or ideas from texts **Reading AF1** Use a range of strategies including accurate decoding of text, to read for meaning **Reading AF4** Identify and comment on the structure and organisation of texts, including grammatical and presentational features at text level **Reading AF5** Explain and comment on writers' uses of language, including grammatical and literary features at word and sentence level	35 36
9. Creating and shaping texts Experiment with different narrative forms and styles to write their own stories Open a story Start with a question The temptation: 1 and 2 Borrow a character	**Open a story** and **Start with a question** help the children to experiment with narrative forms and styles to write their own stories. The children experiment with different story openings. The activities provide opportunities for the children to change the order of material within a paragraph and to consider the effects. You could ask them to compare the effect if the opening is changed: for example, beginning *The Water Horse* with *Kirstie found a 'mermaid's purse' just above the high-tide mark.* Ask them why they think the author preferred to begin *It was Kirstie who found it.* Similarly, the children could consider the effect of changing the opening of *The Sheep-Pig* to *Mrs Hogget heard the very high, very loud, very angry sounding squealing of a pig.* Discuss the effect of beginning, as the author did, with a question. Encourage the children to discuss and note ideas as they experiment with their story openings. **The temptation: 1** and **2** encourage the children to experiment with narrative forms and styles, providing support to help them to write a new scene for a story. They learn from an author about how to use narrative to describe the key features of a scene, to develop a character and to introduce a key event into a story. They can also learn how to create tension from this passage. Here this is achieved through William's thoughts as he reads the notice, considers what might happen if he pulls the communication cord and finally persuades himself that it will be all right if he pulls it only a little. The contrasting short sentences recount what happens after he pulls the cord a little, then a little harder, then much harder. The children could try using this technique in their 'Temptation' story. This activity could be linked with work in citizenship on Choices in which the children focus on the consequences of choices they make. **Borrow a character** helps the children to work independently to plan (and later, write) a complete story with an interesting opening, paragraphs for build-up, climax or conflict, resolution and ending. They build their story around a character they have come across in their reading. They could begin by thinking about a character they know from stories, then imagining him or her in a setting they know is compatible with the character, introducing an event and then considering how this character would respond.	**All Writing AFs, especially:** **Writing AF1** Write imaginative, interesting and thoughtful texts **Writing AF2** Produce texts which are appropriate to task, reader and purpose **Writing AF7** Select appropriate and effective vocabulary	37 38 39–40 41
11. Sentence structure and punctuation Punctuate sentences accurately, including use of speech marks and apostrophes Add a comma Makes a change Conversation poem	**Add a comma** helps the children to understand how to use commas to separate clauses, and to surround a clause to add information to a sentence, in order to make a sentence easier to read and the meaning clear. They could read the sentences aloud with a partner and discuss where there should be a slight pause. This will help them to decide where to place the commas. **Makes a change** helps the children to use punctuation as a powerful tool in expressing meaning. Draw out that by changing the punctuation of a sentence, its meaning can be changed – sometimes to give the complete opposite of what is intended. Makes a change answers: Children – do not drive across playground. Caution! Hot Water! Gents – ready to wear suits. Lions, please stay in your car. Don't throw people below! She was a pretty tall girl. No one knows. Me? Call me, Jim. **Conversation poem** is about recording observations in the form of a dialogue. It provides an opportunity to practise punctuating a dialogue and using capital letters appropriately and could be linked with work in citizenship or science in which the children are encouraged to take notice of all the relevant details before making a judgment.	**Writing AF5** Vary sentences for clarity, purpose and effect **Writing AF6** Write with technical accuracy of syntax and punctuation in phrases, clauses and sentences	42 43 44

Year 5 Narrative Unit 2 – Traditional stories, fables, myths, legends

Activity name	Strand and learning objectives	Notes on the activities	Assessment Focus	Page number
Story spidergram The Three Little … Humpty Dumpty: 1 and 2 Humpty Dumpty words	**1. Speaking** Tell a story using notes designed to cue techniques, such as repetition, recap and humour	**Story spidergram** promotes creativity in storytelling and provides a spidergram that can be used to provide cues to support telling a story, rather than reading it from a written script. It helps to encourage the children to 'enter into the story' as they tell it and requires them to think about it as they do so, rather than focusing on reading it correctly. You could use the CD-ROM to edit the activity, replacing the pictures and captions with others, for a different type of story. The completed page can also be displayed on the interactive white-board for use as an autocue. **Vocabulary:** *alien, character, cue, plot, spidergram.* **The Three Little…** helps the children to adapt the story of The Three Little Pigs to create their own story to tell to younger children. The pictures they choose and their notes can be used as cues for telling a story, rather than reading it from a written script. This encourages them to think about the story as they tell it and adapt it if they think of better ideas as they go. In order to emphasise the speech and performance aspects of the story, discuss the phrases; for example, 'No, no, by the ___ on my ___ I will not let you in' or 'Little little ___ let me come in' and how the children could alter them to match their own versions. You could also discuss stock characters in traditional tales or fairytales, such as the wicked wolf, ogre, witch or monster. Remind the children of common themes such as good and evil, attacker and victim, the weak overcoming the strong. **Vocabulary:** *fairytale, stock character, theme, traditional tale.* **Humpty Dumpty: 1** and **2** and **Humpty Dumpty words** provide a framework for the children's storytelling based on a familiar nursery rhyme. They also suggest how they can begin to adapt it: turning it into a humorous crime story to entertain others of their own age. The ideas for the stories can be as silly as the children like. Encourage them to make notes rather than writing the story, so that they can use these notes as prompts for storytelling, rather than story-reading. They can also play with words as they explore different ways of using words. Recap could involve referring to the nursery rhyme. It will be useful to provide books of phrases and sayings: for example, Brewer's Dictionary of Phrase and Fable (Cassell). Dictionary of Idioms (Linda & Roger Flavell, Kyle Cathie) or The Penguin Dictionary of English Idioms (Daphne M. Gulland & David G. Hinds-Howell, Penguin). **Vocabulary:** *army, audience, cavalry, egghead, egotist, hardboiled, humour, Humpty Dumpty, nursery rhyme, poach, poacher, recap, scramble, scrambled, soft-boiled, soldiers.*	**Speaking and listening AF1** Talk in purposeful and imaginative ways to explore ideas and feelings, adapting and varying structure and vocabulary according to purpose, listeners, and content	45 46 47–49
Negative questions Negative to positive	**2. Listening and responding** Identify different question types and evaluate impact on audience	**Negative questions** and **Negative to positive** focus on identifying negative and positive questions and evaluating their impact on an audience. Like leading questions these invite an expected answer and can make the interviewee feel uncomfortable if he or she does not want to give that response: for example, *Do you like the present my brother gave you?/Don't you like the present my brother gave you? or Can you sing?/Can't you sing?* Explain to the children that negative questions can be used to help to make a point: for example, in the kind of interview that is trying to expose an issue or persuade, negative questions provide emphasis and urgency. Positive questions do not always work as well in all circumstances. During the plenary session invite the children to read some of the questions and answers and describe how the new questions affected the responses (and how the person being questioned felt). The children should notice the difference that is made by changing the questions from negative to positive. **Vocabulary:** *negative question, positive question.*	**Speaking and listening AF4** Understand the range and uses of spoken language, commenting on meaning and impact and draw on this when talking to others	50 51
How does it feel?	**4. Drama** Reflect on how working in role helps to explore complex issues	**How does it feel?** This role-play activity links with PSHE, touching on issues such as bullying and stealing which may need to be handled sensitively. The children are encouraged to explore an issue through role-play, which will lead them to appreciate that while there is no 'right answer', they can gain a deeper understanding of the problem by looking at it from different perspectives.	**Speaking and listening AF3** Create and sustain different roles and scenarios, adapting techniques in a range of dramatic activities to explore texts, ideas, and issues	52
The mad tea party	**4. Drama** Perform a scripted scene making use of dramatic conventions	**The mad tea party** You may wish to begin by reminding the children that plays are written down but they are intended to be performed rather than read. The script gives the directors and actors clues about how to stage the play and role-play about how the characters would move or react to the words of others. Allow an opportunity for the children to perform their scenes to the class.	**Speaking and listening AF3** Create and sustain different roles and scenarios, adapting techniques in a range of dramatic activities to explore texts, ideas, and issues	53
Unstressed vowels: 1 and 2	**6. Word structure and spelling** Spell words containing unstressed vowels	**Unstressed vowels: 1** and **2** develop the children's ability to spell words containing unstressed vowels through using 'spellspeak'. This encourages them to focus on, and therefore remember, the unstressed vowel.	**Writing AF8** Use correct spelling	54–55

Topic	Learning objective	Description	Assessment Focus	Page
Noun converter What's my job? Noun suffixes	**6. Word structure and spelling** Know and use common prefixes and suffixes, e.g. *im-, ir-, -cian*	**Noun converter** helps to consolidate the children's knowledge of the use of the noun suffixes **-ment, -ness, -ity, -tion, -sion, -ssion** and **-age**, how to form a noun from another word and how these suffixes affect the spelling of the base word. **What's my job?** is about spelling patterns. The children learn to recognise suffixes and develop an understanding of how they modify meaning and spelling. It focuses on the suffix **-cian** for forming nouns for people. You could ask the children to write sentences using some of the base words and then their associated **-cian** words. **Noun suffixes** is concerned with spelling patterns. The children learn to recognise noun suffixes and develop an understanding of how they modify meaning and spelling, which can include converting a noun to another noun with a linked but different meaning; for example, friend/friendship, child/childhood. This knowledge can help the children to decode and understand unfamiliar words.	**Writing AF8** Use correct spelling	56 57 58
Fabulous fables	**7. Understanding and interpreting texts** Make notes on and use evidence from across a text to explain events or ideas	**Fabulous fables** focuses on the messages and teaching of Aesop's fables. For a less challenging activity you could supply the messages for the children to match to the fables: *it is sensible to save while you have plenty; a liar is not believed for long; do not let flattery affect your common sense, there is strength in numbers.*	**Reading AF2** Understand, describe, select or retrieve information, events or ideas from texts and use quotation and reference to text **Reading AF3** Deduce, infer or interpret information, events or ideas from texts **Reading AF1** Use a range of strategies including accurate decoding of text, to read for meaning **Reading AF4** Identify and comment on the structure and organisation of texts, including grammatical and presentational features at text level **Reading AF5** Explain and comment on writers' uses of language, including grammatical and literary features at word and sentence level	59
Story sorts Creation myths	**7. Understanding and interpreting texts** Compare different types of narrative and information texts and identify how they are structured	**Story sorts** introduces the different types of traditional stories. Answers: *The Three Little Pigs, The Gingerbread Man, Goldilocks and the Three Bears* (fairytales – old stories that tell of enchantments or unreal incidents that could never really happen, such as bears that live in a house and talk); *The Ant and the Grasshopper, The Lion and the Mouse, The Hare and the Tortoise, The Fox and the Hen* (fables – stories told to teach or give a message about life); *Persephone and the Pomegranate Seeds, King Midas, The Story of Rama and Sita, Jason and the Golden Fleece, The Minotaur, Saint George and the Dragon* (myths – stories that are entirely or mainly fictitious and explain a phenomenon that is not understood or explain a popular belief or religious belief); *Androcles and the Lion, Robin Hood and the Sheriff of Nottingham, King Arthur and the Knights of the Round Table, The Story of the Glastonbury Thorn, King Alfred and the Cakes* (legends – stories about real people or people who are thought by some to have been real, stories that are popularly believed to be historical). **Creation myths** provides an opportunity to explore how a common theme (the creation of the universe) is presented in different stories. Ask the children why they think most religions have creation myths and draw out that many myths develop in order to explain things people do not understand. Some people accept these stories as history but others, including those who belong to that faith group, recognise them as traditional stories to explain the creation (something that even now is not completely understood by scientists). If they have read Rudyard Kipling's *Just-So* stories, they might be able to find similarities between these and myths.	**Reading AF2** Understand, describe, select or retrieve information, events or ideas from texts and use quotation and reference to text **Reading AF3** Deduce, infer or interpret information, events or ideas from texts **Reading AF1** Use a range of strategies including accurate decoding of text, to read for meaning **Reading AF4** Identify and comment on the structure and organisation of texts, including grammatical and presentational features at text level **Reading AF5** Explain and comment on writers' uses of language, including grammatical and literary features at word and sentence level	60 61
	7. Understanding and interpreting texts Explore how writers use language for comic and dramatic effects		**Reading AF2** Understand, describe, select or retrieve information, events or ideas from texts and use quotation and reference to text **Reading AF3** Deduce, infer or interpret information, events or ideas from texts **Reading AF1** Use a range of strategies including accurate decoding of text, to read for meaning **Reading AF4** Identify and comment on the structure and organisation of texts, including grammatical and presentational features at text level **Reading AF5** Explain and comment on writers' uses of language, including grammatical and literary features at word and sentence level	

Activity name	Strand and learning objectives	Notes on the activities	Assessment Focus	Page number
	8. Engaging with and responding to texts Compare the usefulness of techniques such as visualisation, prediction, empathy in exploring the meaning of texts		**All Reading AFs, especially:** **Reading AF6** Identify and comment on writers' purposes and viewpoints and the overall effect of the text on the reader **Reading AF3** Deduce, infer or interpret information, events or ideas from texts **Reading AF7** Relate texts to their social, cultural and historical contexts and literary traditions	
	9. Creating and shaping texts Reflect independently and critically on own writing and edit and improve it		**All Writing AFs, especially:** **Writing AF1** Write imaginative, interesting and thoughtful texts **Writing AF2** Produce texts which are appropriate to task, reader and purpose **Writing AF7** Select appropriate and effective vocabulary	
The rescue plan The rescue: game board The rescue: game cards Legend research The hidden folk	**9. Creating and shaping texts** Experiment with different narrative forms and styles to write their own stories	**The rescue plan** introduces the setting of the legend of Robin Hood and encourages the children to experiment with the narrative form of the legend in planning their own stories. They should first read the legend of Robin Hood. They could also explore the setting through the IWB PowerPoint file *Castle Attack* (see Primary Framework for Literacy: Planning, Year 5 Unit 2 Resources; also the Nottingham Castle website www.bbc.co.uk/nottingham/360/_where to go/castle). It is useful if the children also contribute to a class glossary of castle vocabulary. This could be stored in a table in Word, to allow flexibility in the addition of new head words. These can be added either in their correct alphabetical place (by using Insert Row) or at the end of the table (using Insert row or the Tab key) and sorted alphabetically (by using Sort in the Table menu). A useful reference book is *Castle Diary* by Richard Platt & Chris Riddell (Walker Books). Allow the children time to research the setting – both place and time – before they plan what might happen in the story. **The rescue: game board** and **The rescue: game cards** should be used together to lead to writing in which the children experiment with the narrative form of the legend. The structure of the game board helps the children to plan a story in the form of a legend and, while using this narrative form, to consider details of settings and characters. They could then use a story mountain planning sheet to help them to plan their own episode in the Robin Hood legend. During the game, the children can refer to the legend they know but they are also free to make up some appropriate events if, for example, they land on 'Take a character card' and a settings card. Say what important action the character does there. 'They could write notes as they go along so they remember the sequence of events and the cards chosen. The children collect or lose points as indicated in the circles on the board. The winner is the one with the most points when all players have reached the story ending. The children could use the game to help them to create a setting and characters as well as the plot for a story. These could be keyed in and stored as a multi-layered text. **Legend research** provides an opportunity to experiment with the narrative form and style of a legend. It could be linked with work in history. The extension activity could be completed by all children, with appropriate support. They should first have listened to someone telling the story and identified the ways in which he or she drew in the reader: for example, through varying tone of voice, volume, pace, facial expression and movement. Link this with work in speaking and listening (Telling a story using storytelling techniques). Ask them to record and play back their introduction and to change it where necessary. **The hidden folk** offers an opportunity to experiment with the narrative form and style of a folk-tale. It presents a traditional Icelandic tale written in an uninteresting way and invites the children to retell it so that it sounds more interesting. They can do this by varying the pace through direct and reported speech, portraying action and selecting detail. There is scope for the children to reflect on their writing and edit and improve it. They could introduce additional dialogue into the story to replace some of the reported speech and add exclamations to express Eve's embarrassment at not having washed all her children before God came to visit. They could also present the consequences of Eve's attempted deception through direct speech. The style of the final sentence should reflect the style of many folk-tales: addressing the reader personally to invite him or her to remember the lesson of the story and to believe its consequences. The children might also find it interesting to read real-life stories or events that have been attributed to 'the hidden folk'. (See also *Icelandic Folk and Fairy Tales* by Mary & Hallberg Hallmundsson (Iceland Review). *Icelandic Folktales and Legends* by Jacqueline Simpson (Tempus) and websites such as www.isholf.is/gardar/folk/dolar.htm and www.sbooc.edu/~media/storytelling_links.htm.)	**All Writing AFs, especially:** **Writing AF1** Write imaginative, interesting and thoughtful texts **Writing AF2** Produce texts which are appropriate to task, reader and purpose **Writing AF7** Select appropriate and effective vocabulary	62 63-64 65 66
	10. Text structure and organisation Experiment with the order of sections and paragraphs to achieve different effects		**Writing AF3** Organise and present whole texts effectively, sequencing and structuring information, ideas and events **Writing AF4** Construct paragraphs and use cohesion within and between paragraphs	

Activity name	Strand and learning objectives	Notes on the activities	Assessment Focus	Page number
Storyteller	**11. Sentence structure and punctuation** Adapt sentence construction to different text types, purposes and readers	**Storyteller** helps the children to rewrite a text for a younger audience. It is useful to discuss what should be changed: sentence length, number of verbs/clauses in a sentence and the level of the vocabulary. The children could also key in their altered text and change the font and the size, spacing and layout of the text. The first sentence need not be changed but model how to alter the second sentence: for example, *It was not a fine stick but the kind you could use as firewood.* Some of the longer sentences could be split into two or more short sentences. For example, the final sentence could be split up and simplified as follows: *He picked up a sharp axe to cut off the bark. Then he stopped. A little thin voice seemed to cry out, 'Do not hit me too hard!'*	**Writing AF5** Vary sentences for clarity, purpose and effect **Writing AF6** Write with technical accuracy of syntax and punctuation in phrases, clauses and sentences	67
Recount to dialogue	**11. Sentence structure and punctuation** Punctuate sentences accurately, including use of speech marks and apostrophes	**Recount to dialogue** reinforces the children's understanding of direct and indirect speech and how to punctuate these. Speech marks (also known as quotation marks or inverted commas – although only the opening 'commas' are actually inverted) are used in pairs. In handwriting and many computer fonts the opening and closing marks are differentiated in shape but in some fonts the shape is the same for both. Children are usually taught the traditional usage of double marks (" and " – sometimes referred to as 66 and 99 to remind the children of the orientation of the double, sometimes inverted, commas). It is becoming more common, especially in print, to use single marks, with double marks for quotes within quotes. For example, *Adam said, 'I met the manager, who said, "I shall look into this," but he did not look very hard.'* Other punctuation marks, such as commas, question marks or exclamation marks, are placed within the speech marks (except in American English). Although the quotation might be a complete sentence, the full stop is replaced by a comma if the reporting clause (for example: *said Adam, asked Ella, replied Peter*) follows the quotation – in effect continuing the sentence: *'I'd like you to see this,' said James.* Question marks and exclamation marks are used as in any other sentence: it does not begin a new sentence, even if it follows an exclamation mark or question mark: *'Did you see that?' asked James. 'Come and see this!' called James.* The children could begin by highlighting or underlining the words that are actually spoken. Those who complete the extension activity could perform their play with their groups; this could be linked with work in religious education.	**Writing AF5** Vary sentences for clarity, purpose and effect **Writing AF6** Write with technical accuracy of syntax and punctuation in phrases, clauses and sentences	68

Year 5 Narrative Unit 3 – Stories from other cultures

Activity name	Strand and learning objectives	Notes on the activities	Assessment Focus	Page number
Put yourself in their place: 1 and 2	**4. Drama** Reflect on how working in role helps to explore complex issues	**Put yourself in their place: 1** and **2** link to work in history on the Victorians. The role-play activities allow the children to explore the issue of child labour from historical and social perspectives. Discuss the historical context, explaining that children in the potteries were employed by skilled adult workers, rather than by the pottery owners. As a result, many pottery owners tuned a blind eye to their ill-treatment.	**Speaking and listening AF3:** Create and sustain different roles and scenarios, adapting techniques in a range of dramatic activities to explore texts, ideas, and issues	69-70
Asif's viewpoint: 1 and 2	**9. Creating and shaping texts** Experiment with different narrative forms and styles to write their own stories **9. Creating and shaping texts** Vary pace and develop viewpoint through the use of direct and reported speech, portrayal of action, selection of detail	**Asif's viewpoint: 1** and **2** draw on the children's reading (*Parvana's Journey* by Deborah Ellis). They experiment with a narrative form and style of dialogue to tell the story from a different point of view but, as in the original, in the third person. They should focus on how the situation must have appeared to Asif, the boy who was living in the cave. To help, you could ask questions such as *Would Asif have known Parvana's name? How will you change the story to show how Parvana felt?* It is useful to point out that, instead of Parvana trying to find out about the boy in the cave, Asif would have been trying to find out about the girl outside, for example: 'Get out of my cave!' Asif could hear the girl running away. Then silence. She had stopped. Then he saw her at the mouth of the cave. 'Hello,' she called. Asif called back, 'I told you to get out of my cave!' The children could highlight those parts of the extract which in particular show Parvana's viewpoint. This will act as a visual aid as they write their own version.	**All Writing AFs, especially:** **Writing AF1** Write imaginative, interesting and thoughtful texts **Writing AF2** Produce texts which are appropriate to task, reader and purpose **Writing AF7** Select appropriate and effective vocabulary	71-72
War zone research Letter from a war zone Agra mystery: 1 and 2	**9. Creating and shaping texts** Experiment with different narrative forms and styles to write their own stories	**War zone research** and **Letter from a war zone** help the children to adapt non-narrative forms to help them to write fiction. They find out about a war zone, make notes about the effects the war has on real children and then use their notes to inform narrative writing in the form of a letter. They may find the following websites useful: www.warchild.org.uk and www.christianaid.org.uk/stoppoverty/conflict. It is important to be aware of children in your class and school who may have experienced life in a war zone. The activities require them to consider the appropriate language register for a letter to a pen-friend – informal and personal, using the first person. **Agra mystery: 1** develops the children's skills in researching the setting for a story in a different culture. They adapt non-narrative text to help in writing fiction. Point out that professional fiction writers research and make notes to help them to write in a way that convinces their readers – that research is not only for factual writing. **Agra mystery: 2** focuses on experimenting with a narrative form and using the children's previous non-narrative note-making in order to tell a story. They develop the viewpoint through the use of direct and reported speech, portrayal of action and selection of detail. It is useful to write a sample paragraph as if no research has been done: for example, in which the children are not named and might be playing in a garden when birds fly from a tree (giving no details of what the garden is like, the type of tree, the colours of the birds and so on). Invite the children to develop the description and narrative using the details they found in their research. The children can make their own decision about whether to write a first- or third-person narrative.	**All Writing AFs, especially:** **Writing AF1** Write imaginative, interesting and thoughtful texts **Writing AF2** Produce texts which are appropriate to task, reader and purpose **Writing AF7** Select appropriate and effective vocabulary	73-74 75 76

Activity name	Strand and learning objectives	Notes on the activities	Assessment Focus	Page number
Tell the story Dialogue to recount	**11. Sentence structure and punctuation** Adapt sentence construction to different text types, purposes and readers	**Tell the story** and **Dialogue to recount** introduce indirect speech. Reported speech includes direct speech, in which speech marks are used and the actual words that were spoken are reported, and indirect speech, in which the substance of the spoken words is reported. For example: *Direct speech:* "I fear we are lost," said Rhiannon to Alex. *Indirect speech:* Rhiannon told Alex that she feared they were lost. Both these activities require the children to report speech without using speech marks. They could begin by using a red pen or highlighter to circle or mark the parts they need to change and to insert any extra words which are needed. During the plenary session invite volunteers to read aloud their altered sentences; ask them to point out the parts they changed, and to say why. Discuss why direct and indirect speech are useful in narrative – in combination – and the weaknesses of using only one technique.	**Writing AF5** Vary sentences for clarity, purpose and effect **Writing AF6** Write with technical accuracy of syntax and punctuation in phrases, clauses and sentences	77–78
Two-way sentences Brackets wrap-up	**11. Sentence structure and punctuation** Punctuate sentences accurately, including use of speech marks and apostrophes	**Two-way sentences** helps the children to use punctuation as a powerful tool in expressing meaning. Draw out that by changing the punctuation of a sentence its meaning can be changed – sometimes to give the complete opposite of what is intended. Answers: "Can you juggle, Selma?" asked Dean. "Can you juggle?" asked Selma. "Come and see, Mum," called Amanda. "Come and see, Mum," called Amanda. "I can't draw Miss Lee," said Ben. "I can't draw, Miss Lee," said Ben. Dad said, "Gina was acting stupidly." "Dad," said Gina, "was acting stupidly." "Jason," called Leila from the garden. Jason called Leila from the garden. Nobody answered Lee. "Nobody," answered Lee. "Nobody," answered Lee. **Brackets wrap-up** introduces the uses of brackets as punctuation marks in a sentence. They are always used in pairs. For normal punctuation round brackets are used to surround explanatory or supplementary information which would otherwise interrupt the flow of a sentence. The sentence would make sense without the parenthesis (bracketed part) which in some cases could stand alone as a separate sentence but in others might consist of a single word or a phrase.	**Writing AF5** Vary sentences for clarity, purpose and effect **Writing AF6** Write with technical accuracy of syntax and punctuation in phrases, clauses and sentences	79 80

Year 5 Narrative Unit 4 – Older literature

Activity name	Strand and learning objectives	Notes on the activities	Assessment Focus	Page number
Tune in In trouble!	**2. Listening and responding** Identify some different aspects of talk which vary between formal and informal occasions	**Tune in** provides a structure to help the children to identify some aspects of talk that vary for different audiences – they listen to radio broadcasts intended for different groups of people. They should notice differences in formality as well as vocabulary level and tone of voice. The extension activity could lead to group activities in which the children present something they have learned in their work in another subject, in a way that is accessible to younger children and makes them want to listen. This could include the use of music, songs, sound effects, rhymes, games and so on. They could record a tape or CD for the younger children to listen to. **Vocabulary:** audience, broadcast, listen, radio, style, tone of voice, vocabulary. **In trouble** encourages the children to report situations in different ways to illustrate how language changes according to context. This links closely with text-level work on appropriate language in writing. Invite children to perform their speeches to the class, and discuss features of formal and informal language, such as abbreviations, slang and standard and non-standard English. Children who complete the extension activity could also perform their role-plays to the class.	**Speaking and listening AF4** Understand the range and uses of spoken language, commenting on meaning and impact and draw on this when talking to others	81 82
An older novel	**8. Engaging with and responding to texts** Reflect on reading habits and preferences and plan personal reading goals	**An older novel** provides a reading journal format in which the children can record the main events of a book they read or listen to in serial form. It helps them to record the main events of a chapter, anything that puzzles them or questions they want to ask about it, and their predictions about what might happen. During plenary sessions they could tell the others their questions; encourage the others to suggest answers based on what they know of the story, the setting and the characters. They could also talk about their predictions and give reasons. Encourage the others to question these and give reasons.	**All Reading AFs, especially:** **Reading AF6** Identify and comment on writers' purposes and viewpoints and the overall effect of the text on the reader **Reading AF3** Deduce, infer or interpret information, events or ideas from texts **Reading AF7** Relate texts to their social, cultural and historical contexts and literary traditions	83
Just William	**10. Text structure and organisation** Experiment with the order of sections and paragraphs to achieve different effects	In **Just William** the children read a passage based on a *Just William* story but changed into modern-day English. They are asked to use what they have learned about the language of older stories, and what they know about daily life at the time, to help them to rewrite the paragraph in the style of a *Just William* story.	**Writing AF3** Organise and present whole texts effectively, sequencing and structuring information, ideas and events **Writing AF4** Construct paragraphs and use cohesion within and between paragraphs	84

First table

	11. Sentence structure and punctuation Punctuate sentences accurately, including use of speech marks and apostrophes		AF	Page
Colon leaders Semi-colon connections Apostrophe alert Punctuation program		**Colon leaders** consolidates the children's understanding of how to use colons for separating a sentence into two parts. The part which follows the colon explains or amplifies the part which precedes it. A colon can also be used to introduce a list or series or a long quotation. The parts of a sentence which are separated by a colon depend on one another and would not make sense if they were written as separate sentences. You could also write sentences which require colons on strips of paper, give them to groups of children and ask them to cut the strip where the colon should be. They could then glue the strips onto coloured paper and insert the colons in the gaps. Ask them to read the sentences aloud to check them for sense. **Semi-colon connections** consolidates the children's understanding of how to use semi-colons for linking clauses instead of a conjunction. It can also be used for separating long items in a list, especially where the items in the list contain commas. In this activity where the focus is on linking clauses. During the plenary session you could ask volunteers to read the sentences aloud while the others listen and say where the semi-colon is. Tell them that in these sentences semi-colons are used instead of connective words. The children could reread the sentences inserting a connective word instead of the semi-colon: for example, *I like playing football but most of my friends do not.* **Apostrophe alert** consolidates the children's understanding of the use of the apostrophe to denote ownership (for singular and plural nouns). Note that possessive pronouns, which show ownership, never have apostrophes. It is also important to emphasise that apostrophes are never used for forming plurals. The children could collect examples of other book titles as well as song titles which contain apostrophes. As a further extension activity they could also collect examples of the use of unnecessary apostrophes in plurals and in possessive pronouns: for example, *the 1900's, Buy our apple's – two kilo's for the price of one.* **Punctuation program** provides an opportunity for the children to consolidate their understanding of punctuation marks or for assessment of their learning. After they have completed the activity ask them to compare the results with those of a partner and, during the plenary session, encourage them to discuss any discrepancies.	**Writing AF5** Vary sentences for clarity, purpose and effect **Writing AF6** Write with technical accuracy of syntax and punctuation in phrases, clauses and sentences	85 86 87 88

Year 5 Narrative Unit 5 – Film narrative

	Objective		AF	Page
All cued up In the deep dark wood Gory story	**1. Speaking** Tell a story using notes designed to cue techniques, such as repetition, recap and humour	**All cued up** provides a set of blank cue cards for the children to use for their storytelling notes or for notes on a factual talk, argument or explanation. Instead of using pieces of card they could type their cues and display them on the interactive whiteboard so that they can be used as an 'autocue'. **Vocabulary:** *autocue, cue, humour, recap, repetition.* **In the deep dark wood** … for this activity it may be helpful to revise such aspects of story structure as characters, setting and dialogue. Also discuss how humour is created in the story opening. The children should be encouraged to comment on one another's performances in the plenary session. **Gory story** you could talk about other Roald Dahl stories that the children know, analysing what makes them funny and interesting (for example, they never end in the way you expect).	**Speaking and listening AF1** Talk in purposeful and imaginative ways to explore ideas and feelings, adapting and varying structure and vocabulary according to purpose, listeners, and content	89 90 91
The Piano: scenes The Piano: mood cards The Piano: a life in a tune The Piano: thoughts and words	**7. Understanding and interpreting texts** Infer writers' perspectives from what is written and from what is implied **7. Understanding and interpreting texts** Compare different types of narrative and information texts and identify how they are structured **8. Engaging with and responding to texts** Compare the usefulness of techniques such as visualisation, prediction, empathy in exploring the meaning of texts	**The Piano: scenes** helps the children to discuss their responses to the film *The Piano* by Aidan Gibbons. It provides a series of cards depicting scenes from the film which can be used as prompts to help the children to focus on a particular scene and what it says. After showing the film you could ask the children to put the cards in the order in which they are shown in the film and use them as prompts to help them to tell the story, using a flashback. They could also put them in the order in which they happened and compare this with the order in which they appear in the film. They could write a summary or heading for each scene. **The Piano: mood cards** focuses on the mood and atmosphere of *The Piano*. It also makes the children aware that a story can be told visually without words. Ask them which mood cards they used the most often. Ask them what, in each scene, gave it a particular mood or atmosphere. They could observe one another miming some of these scenes and notice how they use the posture and movements of their bodies and their facial expressions to express a feeling. **The Piano: a life in a tune** suggests some questions to ask the piano player in the film. The answers can be inferred from scenes in the film. During the plenary session ask the children to explain their answers and to give evidence from the film. They could also pose some questions of their own and discuss what the answers might be, and why. **The Piano: thoughts and words** widens the children's understanding of the characters in the film through dramatic techniques as they focus on specific scenes from the film *The Piano* and write two words the characters might say if there were dialogue. Children could 'hotseat' the pianist, to help them think in role, and also do paired role-play to establish the thoughts and words of the characters. As a further extension they could write a monologue (in the first person) for the piano player. They could also write biography of the piano player from the point of view of another character.	**Reading AF2** Understand, describe, select or retrieve information, events or ideas from texts and use quotation and reference to text **Reading AF3** Deduce, infer or interpret information, events or ideas from texts **Reading AF1** Use a range of strategies including accurate decoding of text, to read for meaning **Reading AF4** Identify and comment on the structure and organisation of texts, including grammatical and presentational features at text level **Reading AF5** Explain and comment on writers' uses of language, including grammatical and literary features at word and sentence level **All Reading AFs, especially:** **Reading AF6** Identify and comment on writers' purposes and viewpoints and the overall effect of the text on the reader **Reading AF3** Deduce, infer or interpret information, events or ideas from texts **Reading AF7** Relate texts to their social, cultural and historical contexts and literary traditions	92 93 94 95

Activity name	Strand and learning objectives	Notes on the activities	Assessment Focus	Page number
Evaluator	**9. Creating and shaping texts** Reflect independently and critically on own writing and edit and improve it	**Evaluator** develops the children's skills in reflecting independently and critically on their own writing so that they can edit and improve it. Their short film can be a collection of still images (photographs and drawings) linked by music, spoken words or other devices. They could also create movement through a simple animation either by using special software or by drawing several images with slight differences and showing them in quick succession. They should consider the ways in which colour affects the mood or atmosphere of a scene, the emotions communicated by facial expressions, the ways in which movement can be used to tell a story, indicate the passage of time or communicate feelings, and how sounds can evoke memories, communicate feelings and create an atmosphere. Encourage the children to discuss one another's work – to get input and feedback from other viewers. During the plenary session, ask them for evidence to support their explanations.	**All Writing AFs, especially:** **Writing AF1** Write imaginative, interesting and thoughtful texts **Writing AF2** Produce texts which are appropriate to task, reader and purpose **Writing AF7** Select appropriate and effective vocabulary	96
Is this your life? Life story Biopic	**9. Creating and shaping texts** Experiment with different narrative forms and styles to write their own stories	**Is this your life?** invites the children to consider the key events in a person's life. They could first identify the key events in the life of the main character in the film *The Piano* by Aidan Gibbons and consider how these events are presented (through flashback). They experiment with the form of film narrative to plan their own biographical film about someone they know. This could be linked with work in citizenship on Relationships. It also provides an opportunity for speaking and listening as the children prepare and ask questions and listen to the responses. **Life story** provides a structure to help the children to experiment with a different narrative form and style (an animated film without dialogue) to tell a story of their own. Having identified the five key events in a person's life (see page 100), they devise ways of portraying these as 'snapshots', using 'flashback' techniques and mini-dramas. They first need to have watched the film *The Piano* (see above). The images they select to show on the screen could include photographs, greetings cards (for example, baptism, bar mitzvah, bat mitzvah, amrit ceremony, new job, new home, wedding, birth congratulations, naming ceremony, wedding anniversary). They could also include their own drawings based on the key events. **Biopic** provides a structure to help the children to experiment with a different narrative form and style (animated film without dialogue) to write a story of their own. Having interviewed their subject, selected five key events in the person's life and made notes about how to portray these on screen, the children now consider how these will be presented on screen and how they will be linked: for instance, by music (a piano or another instrument). They will need to consider what they have learned about visual and audio techniques and their effects: music, singing, animation, mini-plays, close-ups, panoramic views, camera angle, panning.	**All Writing AFs, especially:** **Writing AF1** Write imaginative, interesting and thoughtful texts **Writing AF2** Produce texts which are appropriate to task, reader and purpose **Writing AF7** Select appropriate and effective vocabulary	97 98 99
Flagged up Make it agree!	**11. Sentence structure and punctuation** Adapt sentence construction to different text types, purposes and readers	**Flagged up** reinforces the children's understanding of statements and questions. They are required to change declarative sentences into interrogative sentences. During the plenary session ask them to explain what they did to each statement to make it into a question. Focus on the way in which the verb position was changed; for example, *The old house is haunted* becomes *Is the old house haunted?* **Make it agree!** focuses on specific aspects of non-standard English. It is concerned with the agreement of verbs with their subjects.	**Writing AF5** Vary sentences for clarity, purpose and effect **Writing AF6** Write with technical accuracy of syntax and punctuation in phrases, clauses and sentences	100 101
Sentence turn-around Clause squeeze	**11. Sentence structure and punctuation** Punctuate sentences accurately, including use of speech marks and apostrophes	**Sentence turn-around** focuses on the order of words, phrases and clauses in a sentence and the change in meaning which can be created by changing their positions. It helps the children to write unambiguous sentences. During the plenary session the children could explain the two possible meanings of the original sentences, how they changed them and the effects of this change. **Clause squeeze** develops the children's understanding of how to insert a clause into a sentence to add extra information. The shapes show where to insert the clauses. Model how to do this using the completed example and point out the use of who to refer to James, instead of repeating his name. Also point out that the commas before and after the added clause help to communicate the intended meaning and help the reader to read the sentence. Note that a clause always contains a verb. A phrase need not, but can, contain a verb.	**Writing AF5** Vary sentences for clarity, purpose and effect **Writing AF6** Write with technical accuracy of syntax and punctuation in phrases, clauses and sentences	102 103

Year 5 Narrative Unit 6 – Dramatic conventions

Activity name	Strand and learning objectives	Notes on the activities	Assessment Focus	Page number
Bedroom computer: 1 and 2	**1. Speaking** Present a spoken argument, sequencing points logically, defending views with evidence and making use of persuasive language	**Bedroom computer: 1 and 2** help to develop skills in defending views with evidence and provide a basis for presenting a spoken argument. The children should read each statement and think about what it is saying; they can then decide which side of the argument it supports. They can select the ones they think are the most convincing to use in their role-play of an argument between a child and parent or carer about having a computer in their bedroom. To encourage them to think about the argument, they could make notes in the speech bubbles rather than writing the exact words of the points they want to use. They could role-play the argument with others listening to evaluate its effectiveness, including the sequencing of the points. Help the children to appreciate the importance of the sequencing of points made in an argument by trying them in different orders and noticing the difference this makes. The activity links well with work in citizenship on handling conflict. **Vocabulary:** *argument, evidence, facts, opinion, persuade, persuasion, persuasive, role-play, view.*	**Speaking and listening AF1** Talk in purposeful and imaginative ways to explore ideas and feelings, adapting and varying structure and vocabulary according to purpose, listeners, and content	104–105

	2. Listening and responding Identify some different aspects of talk which vary between formal and informal occasions			
Keeping active: 1, 2 and 3	3. Group discussion and interaction Plan and manage a group task over time using different levels of planning	**Keeping active: 1, 2 and 3** provide a structure for managing a group task over time using different levels of planning. Ask the children to decide on group roles, such as leader, scribe and reporter. They begin by suggesting what should be done to keep active, with ideas being collected on the concept map on **Keeping active: 1** but with no discussion of the ideas as yet. They then discuss the ideas and check the facts, before moving on to decide on a plan they can all follow that will help to keep them active (**Keeping active: 2**). This includes checking their progress and making any necessary adjustments to the plan. **Keeping active: 3** provides a format on which they can record the results of their plan and action. These pages can be used to support work in science and PSHE on keeping healthy. **Vocabulary:** *action, active, adjust, collect, concept map, discuss, ideas, leader, improve, plan, report, scribe.*	**Speaking and listening AF2** Listen and respond to others, including in pairs and groups, shaping meanings through suggestions, comments, and question	106–108
Group roles	3. Group discussion and interaction Understand different ways to take the lead and support others in groups	**Group roles** develops the children's understanding of the main roles in a group activity and the language appropriate to them; also their understanding of different ways of taking the lead. They should use these terms when planning other activities. It is useful to rotate these roles so that different children can act as leader, reporter, scribe or mentor. Also make explicit the purpose of each role: leader (start the discussion by asking a question: summarise what has been said); scribe (write notes on the discussion); reporter (report the main points of the discussion, or the group's agreed views on a topic, to the class or another group); mentor (encourage others to speak through using expressions such as *What do you think? Why? Would you like to add anything?*) In any group activity you could draw attention to the roles the children take within their groups. **Vocabulary:** *challenge, collect ideas, decide, describe, encourage, explain, inform, instruct, leader, mentor, opinion, organise, persuade, present, question, reporter, role, scribe, suggest, summarise, support, views.*	**Speaking and listening AF2** Listen and respond to others, including in pairs and groups, shaping meanings through suggestions, comments, and question	109
Cinderella panto: 1 and 2	4. Drama Perform a scripted scene making use of dramatic conventions	**Cinderella: 1** and **2** help the children to consider theatrical effects and how they are achieved, before writing and performing a playscript. Ensure that all the children know the original version of Cinderella and talk about the most memorable characters, then look at how the pantomime adapts the characters to make them comical. Allow an opportunity for groups to perform the scene to their class.	**Speaking and listening AF3** Create and sustain different roles and scenarios, adapting techniques in a range of dramatic activities to explore texts, ideas, and issues	110–111
Pantomime features	4. Drama Use and recognise the impact of theatrical effects in drama	**Pantomime features** is an introduction to the pantomime genre and its theatrical effects. It could lead in to other activities on pantomime (see **Cinderella panto 1** and **2** and **Aladdin playscript. Aladdin characters** and **Model theatre**). Use a video recording of a school pantomime if one is available. Alternatively, show a clip from another source, such as *The Muppet Christmas Carol* or the Blue Peter website (www.bbc.co.uk/cult/classic/bluepeter/simonpetersarah/video/video3.shtml).	**Speaking and listening AF3** Create and sustain different roles and scenarios, adapting techniques to explore texts, ideas, and issues	112
Word history	6. Word structure and spelling Spell words containing unstressed vowels	**Word history** is about irregular spellings and develops the children's knowledge of unstressed vowels and consonants and their understanding of the derivation of words. This can act as a mnemonic – for example, for the **p** in cupboard, the **ea** grapheme for /e/ in breakfast, the **eau** grapheme for /oo/ in beauty and /ow/ in bureau, the **ig** grapheme for /igh/ in sign and the **ough** grapheme for /or/ in naughty (and other words with a similar spelling pattern, such as daughter, slaughter and taught).	**Writing AF8** Use correct spelling	113
Prefix change	6. Word structure and spelling Know and use less common prefixes and suffixes such as im-, ir-, -cian	**Prefix change** develops the children's knowledge of less common prefixes and how to use them to change the meaning of a word. You could edit the page using the CD-ROM: other useful words include *accept, except; again, regain; assure, insure; attain, detain, obtain, retain; attend, extend, intend, pretend; compress, depress, express, impress, oppress, repress, suppress; convict, evict; decathlon, pentathlon; deflate, inflate; deform, inform, reform, transform; disused, misused, unused; emigrant, immigrant; exclude, include; exhale, inhale.* During the plenary session, invite volunteers to make up sentences to illustrate the meanings of both words in each pair.	**Writing AF8** Use correct spelling	114
Segment sense	6. Word structure and spelling Group and classify words according to their spelling patterns and their meanings	**Segment sense** develops the children's knowledge of etymology, thus equipping them to develop personal strategies for learning new words. It focuses on words formed from commonly used word segments from Latin or Greek that occur in many English words. The children could work in small groups to discuss the connection between all the words and, during the plenary session, present their ideas to the class about the meanings of the segments **tele** from the Greek for 'far off', **micro** from the Greek for 'small': **phone** from the Greek for 'sound' or 'voice' and **graph** from the Greek for 'writing'). Possible answers: *telegram, telegraph, telepathy, telephoto, telescope, television; microbe, microchip, microfilm, microphone, microscope, microwave; earphone, headphone, megaphone, microphone, saxophone, videophone, xylophone; autograph, biography, choreograph, grapheme, graphic, paragraph, photograph, radiography.* **Verbalise** focuses on spelling patterns for verbs and develops the children's knowledge of suffixes. The children learn a common verb ending and form verbs from nouns and adjectives, using what they know about changing base word endings. You could link this with work on American spellings. It is helpful if the children sort the verbs into sets on their jotters or individual wipe-off boards before writing the lists on the sheet.	**Writing AF8** Use correct spelling	115
Verbalise				116

Activity name	Strand and learning objectives	Notes on the activities	Assessment Focus	Page number
Script match In the script	**7. Understanding and interpreting texts** Compare different types of narrative and information texts and identify how they are structured	**Script match** develops the children's understanding of what is meant by a script and that television broadcasts that are not fiction can be based on a prepared script (also that some are unscripted but that the spoken words can be recorded afterwards using a transcript). When matching the scripts to the broadcasts they should consider subject language and style of language as well as person and tense. **In the script** develops the children's understanding of the different types and purposes of scripted television broadcasts. Before the activity it is necessary to record different types of television broadcast for the children to watch. After they have completed the activity they could watch the extracts again and notice the different techniques used: one voice or more, sounds such as music or singing, visual effects such as animation, small plays (as in advertisements), panoramic views and so on, and notice the effects of these techniques. Many programmes, e.g. chat shows, cooking programmes, sports commentaries, have unscripted as well as scripted parts. The introductions and endings will almost always be scripted.	**Reading AF2** Understand, describe, select or retrieve information, events or ideas from texts and use quotation and reference to text **Reading AF3** Deduce, infer or interpret information, events or ideas from texts **Reading AF1** Use a range of strategies including accurate decoding of text, to read for meaning **Reading AF4** Identify and comment on the structure and organisation of texts, including grammatical and presentational features at text level **Reading AF5** Explain and comment on writers' uses of language, including grammatical and literary features at word and sentence level	117 118
Leisure survey Leisure documentary planner On screen: 1 and 2	**9. Creating and shaping texts** Adapt non-narrative forms and styles to write fiction or factual texts, including poems	**Leisure survey** and **Leisure documentary** planner help the children to research and plan a non-fiction script. You could introduce it though fiction, in the form of a short play in which a group of children complain about how bored they are because there is nothing to do in their locality and then someone (perhaps a teacher, parent or local council representative) asks them if they are sure there really is nothing to do and challenges them to find out. The audience for the documentary could be other children in the area and other schools. Thinking about the audience will help the children to consider different ways of combining information and style of address, music and so on. **On screen: 1** and **2** encourage the children to adapt narrative and non-narrative forms and styles to write a factual text. They help to scaffold the children's detailed planning and writing of a documentary on leisure facilities in their locality. The task is closely structured but if the children have other ideas about how to make their documentary, they should be encouraged to explore these, too. They begin the activity by writing the script for a mini-play to introduce the theme. This builds on their previous learning about plays and draws on their developing understanding of television scripts (see *100% New Developing Literacy Understanding and Responding to Texts: Ages 9–10*). **On screen: 2** helps the children to consider different ways of writing **On screen: 1** encourages the use of a questioning technique in order to research and present information. When the children evaluate it they should consider how well it makes the audience want to know the information that follows. **On screen: 2** helps the children to make the transition from fiction/drama to non-fiction, factual text. It is useful to remind them of the purpose of a documentary – to present researched facts honestly and in a way that engages the audience's interest. This could include the consideration of bias.	**All Writing AFs, especially:** **Writing AF1** Write imaginative, interesting and thoughtful texts **Writing AF2** Produce texts which are appropriate to task, reader and purpose **Writing AF7** Select appropriate and effective vocabulary	119–120 121–122
Sentence combinations	**11. Sentence structure and punctuation** Punctuate sentences accurately, including use of speech marks and apostrophes	**Sentence combinations** develops the children's understanding of how to construct complex and compound sentences through combining simple sentences using connectives. Point out, however, that it is not always a good thing to write very long sentences. Sometimes short ones are more effective. A simple sentence contains one clause (a main clause); for example, *We shall eat fish and chips for supper*. A compound sentence contains more than one main clause; the clauses have equal value (that is, there are no subordinate clauses); for example, *We shall drink orange juice and eat fish and chips for supper*. A complex sentence (also called a multiple sentence) contains at least one main clause and at least one subordinate clause; for example, *The girl ate the fish and chips which her father had bought for her*. The subordinate clause (underlined) does not make sense as a sentence. A main clause makes sense on its own as a sentence but a subordinate clause depends on the main clause for its meaning.	**Writing AF5** Vary sentences for clarity, purpose and effect **Writing AF6** Write with technical accuracy of syntax and punctuation in phrases, clauses and sentences	123

Year 5 Non-fiction Unit 1 – Instructions

Activity name	Strand and learning objectives	Notes on the activities	Assessment Focus	Page number
Two talks: 1 and 2	**2. Listening and responding** Identify some different aspects of speech which vary between formal and informal occasions	**Two talks: 1** and **2** involve comparing a formal and an informal speech on a similar subject (opening a village fair). The children learn to identify aspects of formal and informal talk: dialect and slang or standard English, contractions or complete clauses, active or passive verbs, first and second or third person. You could read both speeches to the class or invite someone else to read one of them. Ask the children which is the more formal speech, and how they can tell. They could begin with overall impressions and try to justify their comments. Invite them to discuss why the different styles might be used, and how important or not it is to be formal in that context. For **Two talks: 2** it will help if they have a copy of the two speeches for reference. They might need to be reminded of what is meant by first person, second person, third person, active verbs, passive verbs, instruction (command) form of verbs and contractions. **Vocabulary:** *active, command, contraction, dialect, first person, formal, imperative, informal, instruction, passive, second person, slang, third person.*	**Speaking and listening AF4** Understand the range and uses of spoken language, commenting on meaning and impact and draw on this when talking to others	124–125

Activity name	Strand and learning objectives	Notes on the activities	Assessment Focus	Page number
Instruct me Mixed-up instructions	**9. Creating and shaping texts** Adapt non-narrative forms and styles to write fiction or factual texts, including poems	**Instruct me** develops skills in adapting a narrative form and style to write instructions. For a more demanding activity you could scan the text in the box and alter the order of the narrative sentences so that the children are required to put them in order as well as write them in the imperative form. The children should follow each other's instructions to see if they work. They could also explore the software before attempting to rewrite the recount. This will reinforce the value of rehearsing the instructions orally first and help to make sense of the use of instructional/imperative language. **Mixed-up instructions** helps the children to adapt a narrative form and style to write instructions and to put the text in the correct order as well as write them in the imperative form. They also experiment with the order of sentences and change the order of material in a paragraph in order to achieve a logical set of instructions. Having played the game, the children could add some tips for users: for example, how to navigate around the pond, what some of the screen icons mean and where to look for some items they need. Stress that the children should bear in mind the potential audience and that the purpose of the activity is to try to make the instructions clear for those who have never played the game before.	**All Writing AFs, especially:** **Writing AF1** Write imaginative, interesting and thoughtful texts **Writing AF2** Produce texts which are appropriate to task, reader and purpose **Writing AF7** Select appropriate and effective vocabulary	126 127
The instructor	**10. Text structure and organisation** Experiment with the order of sections and paragraphs to achieve different effects **10. Text structure and organisation** Change the order of material within a paragraph, moving the topic sentence	**The instructor** provides an opportunity for the children to write a factual text with a logical order. They write an instructional text using the appropriate form and features and they could cut out and rearrange the notepads to experiment with the order of sentences. Their instructions should take into account the needs of the intended audience.	**Writing AF3** Organise and present whole texts effectively, sequencing and structuring information, ideas and events **Writing AF4** Construct paragraphs and use cohesion within and between paragraphs	128
Formal or informal A closer look Instruction sentences Recount to instruction Make it work!	**11. Sentence structure and punctuation** Adapt sentence construction to different text types, purposes and readers	**Formal or informal** and **A closer look** develop the children's awareness of the need to adapt their writing for different purposes. It is useful to focus on the features which distinguish formal and informal writing, as listed on the chart on page 130. The children could also adapt leaflets or instructions to convert them from formal to informal or from informal to formal text. During the plenary session invite the children to point out the features they changed and to say why. **Instruction sentences** and **Recount to instruction** develop the children's understanding of how sentences work and how to construct an imperative sentence. Note that the imperative or command form of a verb does not necessarily mean that an order is given. It can indicate an instruction or even a request. During the plenary session it is useful to discuss the characteristics of these two different types of sentence. These activities could be linked with work in design and technology in which the children make notes about an artefact or system they have created and then convert these into instructions for someone else to follow. They could pass them to a member of a different group or class to test and evaluate. Recount to instruction could be used to support work in citizenship. **Make it work!** is about branching instructions (instructions in which the sequence depends on the outcomes of each stage of the process). This activity could be linked with problem-solving in science or maths.	**Writing AF5** Vary sentences for clarity, purpose and effect **Writing AF6** Write with technical accuracy of syntax and punctuation in phrases, clauses and sentences	129–130 131–132 133
Making it clear	**11. Sentence structure and punctuation** Punctuate sentences accurately, including use of speech marks and apostrophes	**Making it clear** helps the children to proofread sentences in order to avoid ambiguity. They should decide whether punctuation will help, whether they need to alter the order of some of the words or phrases or whether an extra word or phrase would help.	**Writing AF5** Vary sentences for clarity, purpose and effect **Writing AF6** Write with technical accuracy of syntax and punctuation in phrases, clauses and sentences	134

Year 5 Non-fiction Unit 2 – Recounts

Activity name	Strand and learning objectives	Notes on the activities	Assessment Focus	Page number
Slang match Formal or informal Question time Interview improver	**1. Speaking** Use and explore different question types and different ways words are used, including in formal and informal contexts	**Slang match** draws attention to the differences in vocabulary between formal and informal language. The children could begin by making up sentences using formal language and then consider whether they would say this to their friends or family and, if not, which words they might use instead. It is important to distinguish between slang and swear-words. A few children might not be clear about the differences, especially if they hear people swearing on a regular basis, but by this age they should be able to make a distinction by comparing different types of informal language: for example, that used in the classroom with that used in some situations elsewhere. Teachers will naturally be sensitive in dealing with this if it is likely that children regularly hear members of their families swearing. Some slang will vary from region to region: for example, food (grub, nosh, bait), steal (rob, nick, pinch, half-inch). **Vocabulary:** dialect, formal, informal, language, slang, swear. **Formal or informal** focuses on the different types of language used in formal and informal situations, including forms of address. The children could also list different ways of greeting people or saying goodbye and sort them into 'formal' and 'informal' sets. Another group task to extend the children's learning is to convert a spoken argument (perhaps from one of the previous activities) into a formal and an informal speech. **Vocabulary:** dialect, formal, greeting, informal, polite, slang. **Question time** introduces different types of question (open and closed) and provides examples to help the children to distinguish between them and to become aware of how the form of the question affects the answer. Closed questions usually elicit one or two-word answers, whereas open questions lead to fuller answers that give more detail. You could provide examples of questionnaires that ask different types of question so that the children can see which type is effective for various purposes. **Vocabulary:** answer, ask, closed question, open question, questionnaire.	**Speaking and listening AF4** Understand the range and uses of spoken language, commenting on meaning and impact and draw on this when talking to others	135 136 137

Activity name	Strand and learning objectives	Notes on the activities	Assessment Focus	Page number
		Interview improver develops the children's understanding of open and closed questions. After they have converted the closed questions to open questions, they could compare the possible answers to each version of the question and evaluate the original interview and their altered version of it. When researching any topic, remind them to think about what they want to find out and which type of question would be best: closed questions for easy-to-record factual information and open questions in order to explore reasons and feelings. **Vocabulary:** *answer, ask, closed question, interview, open question, questionnaire, respond, response.*		138
Leading questions Rhetorical questions	**2. Listening and responding** Identify different question types and evaluate impact on audience	**Leading questions** is about questions that lead the interviewee into giving the desired answer. It helps the children to become aware of the ways in which these questions can be used in persuasion. If possible provide recorded interviews (radio or television) in which the interviewer is trying to persuade someone to give particular answers through the use of leading questions. It is useful to discuss with the children whether the use of these questions is fair and how they make the interviewee feel. The following are leading questions because they are based on assumptions and invite a particular answer: *Is it fair that your buying power means small stores can't compete on prices?* (The interviewee would not want to answer 'no', but 'yes' would suggest that he/she does not care about smaller stores), *What about the traffic problems your store has caused since it opened?* and *Would you like cars in front of your house all day and night?* **Vocabulary:** *interview, interviewee, interviewer, leading question.* **Rhetorical questions** introduces the use of rhetorical questions – questions that are used for effect or emphasis and do not require an answer. Another type of question – the 'tag question' is sometimes used in a similar way but it usually invites an expected response, such as yes or no. This involves adding a question such as *isn't it?, does he?, can't you?* to the end of a sentence: for example, *You can speak Urdu, can't you?, Jane went to Turkey, didn't she?* The children could collect examples of rhetorical questions they hear at home, at school or out and about and discuss what the response would be if they answered these questions. You could also collect jokes that involve answering rhetorical questions – the humour usually arises because no answer is expected: for example: Teacher: *What would you say if I came to school with hands as dirty as yours?* Pupil: *I'd be too polite to mention it*, Miss. **Vocabulary:** *rhetorical question.*	**Speaking and listening AF4** Understand the range and uses of spoken language, commenting on meaning and impact and draw on this when talking to others	139 140
Word match game	**2. Listening and responding** Identify some different aspects of speech which vary between formal and informal occasions	**Word match game** helps the children to identify some aspects of language that vary for formal and informal occasions, particularly the use of formal or informal vocabulary. Possible answers: farewell – goodbye, retailing – selling, consume – eat, dispatched – sent, preserved – kept or saved, prepare – get ready, inform – tell, returned – came back or sent back, stated – said, displaying – showing, beverage – drink, dismiss – send away, erroneous – wrong, insert – put in, remarkable – unusual or noticeable, repair – mend or fix, agriculture – farming, credible – believable, entrance – way in, exhibit – show, fracture – break, terminate – end or finish, vegetation – plants, inhabited – lived, connection – link, humorous – funny, circular – round, regretted – was sorry. Answers to extension activity: baby – infant, clap – applaud, choose – elect or select, extra – additional, fun – enjoyment, get – obtain, help – assist, lift – raise, make – manufacture or create, real – genuine, see – observe, stop – terminate or cease. **Vocabulary:** *formal, informal, official, vocabulary.*	**Speaking and listening AF4** Understand the range and uses of spoken language, commenting on meaning and impact and draw on this when talking to others	141
Older people: 1, 2 and 3	**3. Group discussion and interaction** Plan and manage a group task over time using different levels of planning	**Older people: 1, 2** and **3** provide a structure for managing a group task over time using different levels of planning. You could use them in conjunction with work in citizenship on living in a diverse world. The children begin by sorting a set of statements about older people in the community (**Older people: 1**). This is a good opportunity to challenge stereotyped views of older people and for the children to check their assumptions. Remind them of the importance of checking the facts: **Older people: 2** helps with this. Sources of information that the children might use for this include relatives, a social worker who has links with or visits the school and a representative from a local community group or charity or care agency. Once the children have gathered information they can then collect ideas in their group about what they can do. They can then begin to plan the action they can take using **Older people: 3**. Possible actions the children might plan for include visiting and letter-writing or campaigning on behalf of older people. The following websites may help to generate ideas: www.ageconcern.org.uk, www.helptheaged.org.uk/en-gb, www.communitycare.co.uk/Articles/2008/09/29/104087/elderlypeople.html. **Vocabulary:** *answer, campaign, community, discussion, improve, leader, organise, question, research, scribe.*	**Speaking and listening AF2** Listen and respond to others, including in pairs and groups, shaping meanings through suggestions, comments and question	142–144
What's my role?	**3. Group discussion and interaction** Understand different ways to take the lead and support others in groups	**What's my role?** develops the children's understanding of the main roles in a group activity and the language appropriate to them; also their understanding of different ways of taking the lead. They should use these terms when planning other activities. It is useful to rotate these roles so that different children can act as leader, reporter, scribe or mentor. Also make explicit the purpose of each role: leader (start the discussion by asking a question: summarise what has been said); scribe (write notes on the discussion); reporter (report the main points of the discussion, or the group's agreed views on a topic, to the class or another group); mentor (encourage others to speak through using expressions such as *What do you think? Why? Would you like to add anything?*) In any group activity you could draw attention to the roles the children take within their groups. If preferred, **What's my role?** could be adapted for use after a specific group activity so the children can write down what they did in their own group role. **Vocabulary:** *challenge, collect ideas, decide, describe, encourage, explain, inform, instruct, leader, mentor, opinion, organise, persuade, present, question, reporter, role, scribe, suggest, summarise, support, views.*	**Speaking and listening AF2** Listen and respond to others, including in pairs and groups, shaping meanings through suggestions, comments, and question	145

				Page
Group chaos: 1 and 2	**3. Group discussion and interaction** Understand the process of decision making	**Group chaos: 1** and **2** focus on the process of decision-making. Through discussion of the way in which the group in this scenario works, the children can spot the mistakes and identify what should be done. This can be easier than making suggestions about how to make a decision without a concrete starting point. The children could identify the following facts that need to be found out: whether Mrs Taylor has a garden, whether it has any trees and whether she prefers a sunny or shady garden; whether she likes reading and, if so, what types of book she reads; whether she would enjoy a pantomime and, if so, how many tickets would be needed; whether she has plenty of scarves and gloves – she might not have felt cold on the day William saw her without them, or she may have forgotten them. You could use the CD-ROM to adapt the pages so that the children can work on a real decision making task. **Vocabulary:** agree, decision, disagree, problem, progress, solve, summary, task.	**Speaking and listening AF2** Listen and respond to others, including in pairs and groups, shaping meanings through suggestions, comments, and question	146–147
Word-maker The prefix a- Word challenge Transfixed Interaction	**6. Word structure and spelling** Know and use less common prefixes and suffixes, such as im-, ir-, -cian	**Word-maker** develops the children's knowledge of a range of prefixes and suffixes, including less common ones, and their knowledge of spelling patterns. They use spelling rules to help them to add prefixes and/or suffixes to base words. Possible answers (main activity): acceptable, acceptance, accepted, accepting, unacceptable; accessed, accessible, accessing, accession, inaccessible; achievable, achieved, achievement, achieving, unachievable: acted, acting, action, actor, exact, exacted, exacting, react, reacted, reacting, reaction, reactor: agreeable, agreed, agreeing, agreement, disagree, disagreeable, disagreed, disagreeing, disagreement: available, unavailable; changeable, changed, changing, exchange, exchanged, exchanging, unchangeable, unchanging; coded, coding, decode, decoded, decoding; confident, confidence, confident, confiding; differed, difference, different, differing, indifference, indifferent; conduct, conducted, conducting, conduction, conductor, deduct, deduction, deductible, induction, reduction; disobedience, disobey, disobeyed, disobeying, obedience, obeyed, obeying; opened, opening, reopen, reopened, reopening, unopened; apart, compartment, depart, departed, departing, department, departure, impart, imparted, imparting, parted, parting; appliance, applied, apply, applying, compliance, compiled, comply, complying, implied, imply, implying, replied, reply, replying; compress, compressed, compressing, compression, depress, depressed, depressing, depression, express, expressed, expressing, expression, impress, impressed, impressing, impression, pressed, pressing, pressure, repress, repressed, repressing, repression; irrational, rational, rationed, rationing; irregular, irregularity, regularity; nonsense, nonsensical, sensation, sensed, sensible, sensing, sensor; ashamed, shamed, shameful, shaming; awake, waken; (extension activity) inexpressible, irrepressible, reawaken, unimpressed; departmental, irrationality, unacceptability, unavailability. **The prefix a-** and **Word challenge** help the children to learn prefixes, including the less common prefix a-. Most prefixes do not change the spelling of the base word but when a- is added to a word it often doubles the first letter: for example, accelerate, accompany, apply, arrange, assorted, assure, attach. This prefix can have several meanings: on, onto, to, towards, in, up, out, off, from, into. A fairly detailed dictionary, such as the Shorter Oxford or Concise Oxford Dictionary, is needed for page 150. **Transfixed** and **Interaction** help the children to learn common spelling rules and less common prefixes. They should be able to deduce that **trans-** means across and **inter-** means among or between. Neither changes the spelling of the base word. As an extension activity to page 152, ask the children to explain the meaning of the word Internet and suggest why it is a suitable name. The children could write a short story using all the **inter** words on the page, perhaps about an international sports tournament or an intercontinental cultural exchange. The story need not make sense but all the words should be used correctly.	**Writing AF8** Use correct spelling	149–150 151–152
Word groups Partners	**6. Word structure and spelling** Group and classify words according to their spelling patterns and their meanings	**Word groups** focuses on grouping and classifying words by their meanings. These pages could be edited using the CD-ROM. Other useful word groups for page 153 include audio – audible, audition, auditorium, inaudible; graphic – autograph, grapheme, photograph, telegraph; heart – dishearten, hearten, heartfelt, hearty; mine – miner, mineral, mining, undermine; phonics – phoneme, phonetic, stereophonic, telephone; serve – disservice, servant, service, servitude: terminal – exterminate, terminate, termination, terminus; vision – televise, television, visible, visual. **Partners** is about grouping and classifying words according to spelling patterns. It helps the children to use analogy to help them to read and spell untamiliar words. You could use the CD-ROM to edit the page to help the children to read and spell topical words or words they are going to come across in a shared text.	**Writing AF8** Use correct spelling	153
	7. Understanding and interpreting texts Make notes on and use evidence from across a text to explain events or ideas		**Reading AF2** Understand, describe, select or retrieve information, events or ideas from texts and use quotation and reference to text **Reading AF3** Deduce, infer or interpret information, events or ideas from texts **Reading AF1** Use a range of strategies including accurate decoding of text, to read for meaning **Reading AF4** Identify and comment on the structure and organisation of texts, including grammatical and presentational features at text level **Reading AF5** Explain and comment on writers' uses of language, including grammatical and literary features at word and sentence level	154

19

Activity name	Strand and learning objectives	Notes on the activities	Assessment Focus	Page number
Recount chronology: 1 and 2 Recount features	**7. Understanding and interpreting texts** Compare different types of narrative and information texts and identify how they are structured	**Recount chronology: 1** and **2** develop the children's awareness that a recount should present events so that the order in which they took place is clear although it might not begin with the first event. It also develops their awareness of how quotations and reported speech are used. **Recount features** provides a format to help the children to identify the key features of a recount. It is based on the recount *Village Oak Mystery* (page 155) but it could be adapted for analysing other recounts. The children learn that the structure of a recount includes the use of an introduction to orientate the readers and make them want to read on and a summary to indicate what might happen as a result of the events or to explain something. They also learn how quotations from eye-witnesses enliven a recount and demonstrate its reliability.	**Reading AF2** Understand, describe, select or retrieve information, events or ideas from texts and use quotation and reference to text **Reading AF3** Deduce, infer or interpret information, events or ideas from texts **Reading AF1** Use a range of strategies including accurate decoding of text, to read for meaning **Reading AF4** Identify and comment on the structure and organisation of texts, including grammatical and presentational features at text level **Reading AF5** Explain and comment on writers' uses of language, including grammatical and literary features at word and sentence level	155–156 157
Interviews to recount: 1 and 2	**9. Creating and shaping texts** Adapt non-narrative forms and styles to write fiction or factual texts, including poems **10. Text structure and organisation** Experiment with the order of sections and paragraphs to achieve different effects	**Interviews to recount: 1** and **2** develop the children's understanding of the differences between reported and direct speech and writing in paragraphs appropriately, using connectives to improve the flow of their writing. The activities present examples in order to help the children to compose questions that elicit the most information about a topic and to write a recount. The children learn how to incorporate quotations from eye-witnesses to enliven a recount and demonstrate its reliability. They also learn how to structure a recount to include an introduction to orientate the readers and make them want to read on and a summary to indicate what might happen as a result of the events or to explain something. It is useful if they have first completed the activities in the Recounts section of *100% New Developing Literacy Understanding and Responding to Texts: Ages 9-10*.	**All Writing AFs, especially:** **Writing AF1** Write imaginative, interesting and thoughtful texts **Writing AF2** Produce texts which are appropriate to task, reader and purpose **Writing AF7** Select appropriate and effective vocabulary **Writing AF3** Organise and present whole texts effectively, sequencing and structuring information, ideas and events **Writing AF4** Construct paragraphs and use cohesion within and between paragraphs	158–159
News summary	**11. Sentence structure and punctuation** Adapt sentence construction to different text types, purposes and readers	**News summary** helps the children to recognise the essential points in a text. They are asked to write a sentence to summarise a paragraph from a news item. They could work with a partner to discuss which are the most important points in each paragraph. Compare the results at the end and ask the children to justify why they kept some points but not others.	**Writing AF5** Vary sentences for clarity, purpose and effect **Writing AF6** Write with technical accuracy of syntax and punctuation in phrases, clauses and sentences	160
Headline to sentence Rose conversation	**11. Sentence structure and punctuation** Punctuate sentences accurately, including use of speech marks and apostrophes	**Headline to sentence** encourages the children to write sentences based on headlines which give the bare facts (but not in complete sentences). This could be stored sentences developed from the headlines. The children could also make up complete stories developed from the headlines. **Rose conversation** is about recording observations in the form of a dialogue. They provide an opportunity to practise punctuating a dialogue and using capital letters appropriately and could be linked with work in citizenship or science in which the children are encouraged to take notice of all the relevant details before making a judgment.	**Writing AF5** Vary sentences for clarity, purpose and effect **Writing AF6** Write with technical accuracy of syntax and punctuation in phrases, clauses and sentences	161 162

Year 5 Non-fiction Unit 3 – Persuasive writing

Activity name	Strand and learning objectives	Notes on the activities	Assessment Focus	Page number
Come out to play Is that a fact? Sport at school: 1 and 2	**1. Speaking** Present a spoken argument, sequencing points logically, defending views with evidence and making use of persuasive language	**Come out to play** encourages the children to generate, plan and present a persuasive argument against the points presented on the page and to use evidence to support their argument. They should use facts (and check that they are accurate) to defend their argument. Help the children to appreciate the importance of the sequencing of points made in an argument by trying them in different orders and noticing the difference this makes. Like many other activities in this section, this one links well with work in citizenship on children's rights and handling conflict. The children could key in their notes and display the pages on the interactive whiteboard to provide an autocue. **Vocabulary:** *argument, evidence, facts, opinion, persuade, persuasion, persuasive, reason, view.* **Is that a fact?** is about defending views with evidence. The children should decide which statements are true facts. This involves looking up and checking those they are not sure of. You could provide leaflets from health centres or pharmacies or from selected websites: for example, the British Heart Foundation www.bhf.org.uk, Patient UK www.patient.co.uk, BBC health www.bbc.co.uk/health/healthy_living, Direct Gov www.direct.gov.uk/en/HealthAndWellbeing/HealthyLiving, TeacherNet www.teachernet.gov.uk/wholeschool/healthyliving or Cancer Research UK www.cancerresearchuk.org. **Vocabulary:** *accurate, argument, fact, opinion, opposite, persuade, persuasion, persuasive, research, view.*	**Speaking and listening AF1** Talk in purposeful and imaginative ways to explore ideas and feelings, adapting and varying structure and vocabulary according to purpose, listeners, and content	163 164

Title	Objective	Notes	Assessment focus	Page
Sport at school: 1 and 2		**Sport at school: 1** and **2** help the children to plan and present a spoken argument, defending views with evidence and making use of persuasive language. After reading the statements about another school's sports provision they should write statements about provision at their own school, ensuring that the facts are accurate. They can then discuss any changes they would like to see and carry out some research about what is available, using the statements in **Sport at school: 1**, and they could, as a starting point, find out what other schools do. **Sport at school: 2** helps them to introduce the argument, sequence the points they want to make, list facts to support their suggestions, make a note of any persuasive language that might help and summarise their argument. **Vocabulary:** argue, argument, clearly, evidence, finally, firstly, however, ideas, improve, listen, opinions, persuade, persuasion, secondly, so, speech, suggestion, summarise, surely, thus, views.		165–166
And now the news…	**2. Listening and responding** Identify some different aspects of speech which vary between formal and informal occasions	**And now the news** … in this activity the children watch an informal news report and a more formal one, commenting on the differences. It may be helpful to highlight examples of passive verbs and slang on the activity sheet ('was rescued', 'fed up', 'great'). During the plenary, discuss the differences between the two news reports and the reasons for them, with reference to audience and purpose.	**Speaking and listening AF4** Understand the range and uses of spoken language, commenting on meaning and impact and draw on this when talking to others	167
I have a dream: 1 and 2 Come and buy: 1 and 2 Persuaders	**2. Listening and responding** Analyse the use of persuasive language	**I have a dream: 1** and **2** are about persuasive speech. You could first give the children some information about Martin Luther King, or ask them to listen to the speech and to say what they think he was trying to do – and then tell them about his background. The children could listen to the actual speech on the Internet: www.mlkonline.net/dream.html http://media.valenciacc.edu/speech/MLK I Have A Dream.wmv http://sixminutes.dlugan.com/2009/01/18/speech-analysis-dream-martin-luther-king http://www.americanrhetoric.com/speeches/mlkihaveadream.htm. There are also links on YouTube. Ask them how Martin Luther King emphasised his message. The children should notice the repetition of words such as *I have a dream*. *Let freedom ring* and *Free at last* and the dramatic and evocative language that helps the audience to envisage places (also the use of contrast in the following: *…sweltering with the head of injustice, sweltering with the head of oppression. … an oasis of freedom and justice; not by the colour of their skin but by the content of their character.* Draw attention to the powerful images of equality that he creates through language: *all men are created equal; sit down together at the table of brotherhood.* Also note images of people being united: *little black boys and black girls will be able to join hands with little white boys and white girls as sisters and brothers, sit down together at the table of brotherhood, we will be able to join hands and sing.* **Vocabulary:** equality, image, persuade, persuasion, persuasive, recap, repetition, united, unity. **Come buy: 1** and **2** help the children to analyse the use of persuasive speech. After listening to the poem they could talk about the words the goblins used to describe the fruit, making it sound too luscious to resist, and how Laura found their persuasive language irresistible, despite her sister's commonsense warnings and her scared and foreboding tone of voice. You could link this with work in citizenship and PSHE on making choices and keeping safe and healthy, with particular reference to peer pressure or advertising. The entire poem 'Goblin Market' can be found in *The New Oxford Book of Children's Verse* (edited by Neil Philip, OUP). **Vocabulary:** enticing, exciting, foreboding, inviting, persuasive, tone of voice, warning. **Persuaders** is about analysing the use of persuasive speech. The children need to watch an extract from a television programme in which someone tries to persuade another to do something. They should look for ways in which the persuader makes the action seem inviting and irresistible or suggests that it will make the other person special or admirable in some way, or to be envied; they could also look for language that suggests that the person is weak, foolish or stupid for not doing what the persuader wants. A possible follow-up to this work would be for the children to role-play some persuasive scenes to try out different techniques. Ideas might include: persuade a partner to give up watching television; persuade a teacher to give you double playtime; persuade a partner that you would be a good headteacher; persuade a partner to support a different football team; persuade an adult to give up tea and coffee; persuade a partner that you are going to train as a clown for your future career; persuade a partner to believe that spaghetti grows on trees, or that baked beans are found in mines, or that Snow White and the Seven Dwarfs were real people. **Vocabulary:** bold type, emphasise, italics, meaning, stress, underline.	**Speaking and listening AF4** Understand the range and uses of spoken language, commenting on meaning and impact and draw on this when talking to others	168–169 170–171 172
Holiday hints Listen carefully	**3. Group discussion and interaction** Understand different ways to take the lead and support others in groups	**Holiday hints** involves working together to present information in a logical way, and highlights the need for a group leader, or chairperson. Provide an opportunity for the groups to give their talks. **Listen carefully** focusses on the role of the chairperson and links to work in PSHE. Discuss with the children what they think the characteristics of a good chairperson would be.	**Speaking and listening AF2** Listen and respond to others, including in pairs and groups, shaping meanings through suggestions, comments, and question	173 174
Shades of meaning Raise that cash	**3. Group discussion and interaction** Understand the process of decision making	**Shades of meaning** involves making decisions as a group. Model examples of synonyms with different shades of meaning: for example, lies and fibs. This activity could lead to some interesting work on character description: first using words with positive connotations, and then using the equivalent words with negative connotations to describe the same character. **Raise that cash** the children will need to work co-operatively within the group to focus on the decisions to be made and how to reach them. You may need to handle discussions sensitively if some children have links to particular charities (such as cancer charities). If possible, hold a fund-raising day to enable the children to carry out their plans.	**Speaking and listening AF4** Understand the range and uses of spoken language, commenting on meaning and impact and draw on this when talking to others	175 176

Activity name	Strand and learning objectives	Notes on the activities	Assessment Focus	Page number
A different bias: 1 and 2	**7. Understanding and interpreting texts** Infer writers' perspectives from what is written and from what is implied	**A different bias: 1 and 2** present similar facts written from opposing points of view in order to help the children to distinguish between fact and opinion and to recognise bias in writing. They should compare the connotations of words (compare *harmless tricks* with *bullying and blackmail*, *annual fun night* with *sinister practice*, *small gifts of goodies* with *sackfuls of sickly chocolate and amazing outfits with identities disguised*). They should also notice the contrasting adjectives used in each report: 1) fun, harmless, exciting, amazing; 2) threatened, scared, callous, disguised, evil, sickly, tooth-rotting, sinister. In the second report the children should also notice the use of contrast and comparison to suggest that what looks harmless and fun is, in fact, evil and harmful.	**Reading AF2** Understand, describe, select or retrieve information, events or ideas from texts and use quotation and reference to text **Reading AF3** Deduce, infer or interpret information, events or ideas from texts **Reading AF1** Use a range of strategies including accurate decoding of text, to read for meaning **Reading AF4** Identify and comment on the structure and organisation of texts, including grammatical and presentational features at text level **Reading AF5** Explain and comment on writers' uses of language, including grammatical and literary features at word and sentence level	177–178
Dear Editor: 1 and 2 Persuasive language	**7. Understanding and interpreting texts** Explore how writers use language for comic and dramatic effects	**Dear Editor: 1 and 2** help the children to identify the devices used in letters to persuade readers to do something or to agree with a point of view. The children should also notice the structure of the letters: the first paragraph introduces the topic and presents the writer's views (albeit with bias); subsequent paragraphs present the argument in a persuasive way and sometimes as if they are facts); and the final paragraph summarises the argument. It is useful first to ensure that the children understand the terms used: *fact, bias, sequencing, main points, comparison, opinion, appealing, values*. **Persuasive language** focuses on the use of powerful and sometimes emotive vocabulary in advertisements as well as devices such as half-truths, rhetorical questions and ambiguity. You will need to explain these terms, using examples, and to remind the children of their previous learning about verbs, adjectives and connectives. They could also use this chart to help them to identify these features in other advertisements.	**Reading AF2** Understand, describe, select or retrieve information, events or ideas from texts and use quotation and reference to text **Reading AF3** Deduce, infer or interpret information, events or ideas from texts **Reading AF1** Use a range of strategies including accurate decoding of text, to read for meaning **Reading AF4** Identify and comment on the structure and organisation of texts, including grammatical and presentational features at text level **Reading AF5** Explain and comment on writers' uses of language, including grammatical and literary features at word and sentence level	179–180 181
Professor Phake's lecture The persuader Pigeons: 1 and 2	**10. Text structure and organisation** Experiment with the order of sections and paragraphs to achieve different effects	**Professor Phake's lecture** helps the children to experiment with the order of paragraphs to achieve a persuasive effect. It develops skills in using persuasive language in linking ideas in a persuasive text. Having written Professor Phake's lecture, the children could practise reading it aloud with a friend and then a volunteer could be invited to present the lecture to the class, who could vote on the question of whether it persuades them that there is life on Mars. Remind them of the importance of tone of voice (and changes in tone, pitch and volume) when they present or evaluate a talk. **The persuader** helps the children to construct an argument in note form to persuade others of a point of view and then to experiment with the order of paragraphs to achieve a persuasive effect and to construct an argument to persuade. It also consolidates letter-writing skills from previous years and encourages the children to group ideas in paragraphs. For a more challenging activity, ask them to write up their notes in a logical order without cutting them out and physically arranging them. This also provides an opportunity to remind them of letter writing conventions and to discuss the appropriate style of language for this type of letter. It could be linked with work in citizenship (Taking part – developing skills of communication and participation). **Pigeons: 1 and 2** provide an opportunity for the children to adapt persuasive writing for a purpose, to experiment with the order of paragraphs and to present some researched facts to use in a persuasive text. Encourage them to use persuasive devices such as rhetorical questions (for example, *Do you want to be guilty of causing injuries and suffering to pigeons as they fly into sharp wire or become entangled on coils of wire? The town council pays for rubbish left by humans and their dogs to be cleaned up, so what is wrong with cleaning up after pigeons? Are we going to discourage people from coming into the town centre, too?*) Speaking and listening skills are developed as the children plan and present a talk and the others listen and then present counter-arguments, stressing different facts. They should consider how they present the talk: for example, when to look up from the script, making eye contact with the audience, using body language, changing their tone of voice. It can be linked with work in citizenship (Animals and us; Local democracy for young citizens).	**Writing AF3** Organise and present whole texts effectively; sequencing and structuring information, ideas and events **Writing AF4** Construct paragraphs and use cohesion within and between paragraphs	182 183 184–185
Sacks of sentences Persuaders Catchy ads Ghostly persuasion	**11. Sentence structure and punctuation** Adapt sentence construction to different text types, purposes and readers	**Sacks of sentences** consolidates the children's understanding of the different types and purposes of sentences: • statement (a declarative sentence: that is, one which communicates information) • interrogative (asking a question) • imperative/command/instruction (giving an instruction or requesting action to be taken) • exclamation (expressing feelings). During the plenary session, invite volunteers to describe the differences between each type of sentence. Focus on word order, the position, form and tense of the verb, and punctuation.	**Writing AF5** Vary sentences for clarity, purpose and effect **Writing AF6** Write with technical accuracy of syntax and punctuation in phrases, clauses and sentences	186

	Page number
Persuaders focuses on the use of persuasive words and phrases. Discuss the effect of these: for example, the use of *surely* or *without a doubt* gives the effect that the sentence is communicating a fact and makes the reader feel as if he or she *should* do something.	187
Catchy ads reinforces the children's understanding of rhyme and alliteration and focuses on how these can be effective in advertisements. The children could also analyse advertisements they find in newspapers or on the television or radio and describe the features they use for influencing people.	188
Ghostly persuasion helps the children to adapt a non-narrative form and style to write a persuasive text. They use persuasive techniques such as opinions presented as facts, half-truth and bias in order to persuade the readers either that ghosts should be allowed to haunt people or that this should be banned. Point out that the same dialogue can be used to support either opinion. The children could also use this page as a starting point for a group or class debate about whether ghosts should be allowed to haunt people. They should read the quotations and then form their own opinion (or you could ask half the class to argue for the ghosts and the other half for the spook police). They can then use the arguments that best suit their purpose. Remind them of useful persuasive phrases such as *surely, clearly, any right-thinking person, anyone with any common sense, it stands to reason, no one doubts* and rhetorical questions like *What is the problem? Who could doubt...?* This can be linked with work in speaking and listening (Group discussion and interaction).	189

Year 5 Poetry Unit 1 - Poetic style

Activity name	Strand and learning objectives	Notes on the activities	Assessment Focus	Page number
Robert Louis Stevenson Grace Nichols	**7. Understanding and interpreting texts** Infer writers' perspectives from what is written and from what is implied	**Robert Louis Stevenson** presents two poems by Robert Louis Stevenson, who was born and grew up in Scotland in the nineteenth century. He suffered from illness throughout his childhood and was often confined to bed but his nurse told him stories of far-off places that fired his imagination and made him want to travel (which he did later). The poems give some indication of Stevenson's childhood and his interest in travel. Some of the words and phrases indicate his Scottish heritage and the time he lived in: counterpane (a word now rarely used for a bed cover) and kirk (a Scottish word for a church). Draw the children's attention to the regular rhyme patterns of these poems and the descriptive language and the jogging narrative rhythm; the poet sets out to describe imagined scenes through nouns and adjectives, with verbs in the first person that express his interaction with the scenes he imagines. The children could compare the poems with anything they imagine about everyday scenes or situations. **Grace Nichols** presents two poems by Grace Nichols, a contemporary poet from Guyana (now living in Britain). The poems give some indication of her interests: everyday life and the power of nature, both of which she observes in detail. Some of the observations give an indication of her home country: village life that includes a donkey and a market bus, hurricanes and hibiscus. Draw the children's attention to the absence of any particular rhyme pattern in these poems: 'Sea Timeless Song' has no rhyme and 'Early Country Village Morning' has an irregular rhyme pattern (in the first verse the first two lines rhyme; in the second there is no rhyme and in the third verse the second and fourth lines rhyme). Draw attention to the rhythms of the poems: 'Early Country Village Morning' seems to gather strength as the village wakes up, whereas 'Sea Timeless Song' has the rhythm of the tide. Also note the use of onomatopoeia (clip-clopping, yawn) and personification (the sun yawns and pushes darkness out of her eye as if rubbing a sleepy eye on awakening). In the second verse the alliteration of the s sounds suggests the sound of the sea washing in and out on a shore and the repetition of sea timeless creates an impression of timelessness.	**Reading AF2** Understand, describe, select or retrieve information, events or ideas from texts and use quotation and reference to text **Reading AF3** Deduce, infer or interpret information, events or ideas from texts **Reading AF1** Use a range of strategies including accurate decoding of text, to read for meaning **Reading AF4** Identify and comment on the structure and organisation of texts, including grammatical and presentational features at text level **Reading AF5** Explain and comment on writers' uses of language, including grammatical and literary features at word and sentence level	190 191
Researching a poet Free verse: 1 and 2	**7. Understanding and interpreting texts** Explore how writers use language for comic and dramatic effects	**Researching a poet** helps the children to identify key aspects of a poet's style. It can be used with pages 190 and 191 or in connection with the work of other poets. Children could also write a 'style guide' for a poet, summarising that poet's style. Children in the class could research several different poets. See the Children's Poetry Archive at http://www.poetryarchive.org/childrensarchive/home.do for other ideas. **Free verse: 1** and **2** develop the children's understanding of free verse by drawing their attention to the key features of a poem in this style. Draw their attention to the lengths of the lines and the rhythm of the poem. The lines are of varying lengths with no regular pattern and it reads like a monologue in prose, although it is set out in lines, unlike prose, which is continuous. The powerful images the poem conjures up are created through the dog metaphor. The word dog is not used but the children should easily recognise the metaphor from the nouns, verbs and adjectives: (nouns) leash, head, eyes, tongue, tail, legs; (verbs) run, whimpered, panting, looked; (adjectives) frightened, confused. Ask them how the poem makes them feel (they might already have expressed this through exclamations while reading it). Ask the children how the poem is different from their stories based on the poem. They should notice the layout and how this affects the way in which they read the poem. Invite feedback with a volunteer reading the prose passage aloud and another reading the poem.	**Reading AF2** Understand, describe, select or retrieve information, events or ideas from texts and use quotation and reference to text **Reading AF3** Deduce, infer or interpret information, events or ideas from texts **Reading AF1** Use a range of strategies including accurate decoding of text, to read for meaning **Reading AF4** Identify and comment on the structure and organisation of texts, including grammatical and presentational features at text level **Reading AF5** Explain and comment on writers' uses of language, including grammatical and literary features at word and sentence level	192 193–194

Activity name	Strand and learning objectives	Notes on the activities	Assessment Focus	Page number
Build a poem Early morning Free verse	**9. Creating and shaping texts** Adapt non-narrative forms and styles to write fiction or factual texts, including poems	**Build a poem** develops from a poem by Robert Louis Stevenson which is featured in *100% New Developing Literacy Understanding and Responding to Texts: Ages 9–10* (page 52). The children should notice the theme of the poem and the regular rhyme pattern; also the use of verbs in the first person to express his interaction with the scene the poet imagines he is building. The children build their own 'Block City' and then describe it in a verse. Allow time for them to 'play with ideas and words' before they begin writing. They can then make a note of the words and phrases they think sound the best. Evaluation is encouraged in the extension activity so that the children can check their poems for sense, mood and atmosphere as well as the rhyme pattern. **Early morning** provides an opportunity for the children to adapt a non-narrative form (poetry) to write their own verse. It presents a poem by Grace Nichols, a contemporary poet from Guyana now living in Britain (see also *100% New Developing Literacy Understanding and Responding to Texts: Ages 9–10* (page 53). Draw the children's attention to the irregular rhyme pattern (in the first verse the first two lines rhyme; in the second there is no rhyme and in the third verse the second and fourth lines rhyme). Also point out the rhythm, which seems to gather strength as the village wakes up. Also worth noting is the use of onomatopoeia (*clip-clopping, yawn*) and personification (the sun *yawns* and *pushes* darkness out of *her* eye as if rubbing a sleepy eye on awakening). It is useful to prepare for the children's writing beforehand by asking them to notice the place where they live 'waking up' and to make notes and perhaps to take photographs using a digital camera, which could be downloaded and displayed on an interactive whiteboard. Sound recordings could also be made and incorporated into the presentation. **Free verse** develops the children's appreciation of free verse by presenting an example for them to use as a model (see also *100% New Developing Literacy Understanding and Responding to Texts: Ages 9–10* (page 55) for an activity based on the same poem but which draws the children's attention to the key features of this style). They should notice the lengths of the lines and the rhythm of the poem. The lines are of varying lengths with no regular pattern and the poem reads like a monologue in prose, although it is set out in lines, unlike prose, which is continuous. The powerful images the poem conjures up are created through the dog metaphor. The word dog is not used but the children should easily recognise the metaphor from the nouns, verbs and adjectives: (nouns) *leash, eyes, tongue, head, tail, legs*; (verbs) *looked, panting, run, whimpered*; (adjectives) *frightened, confused*. Here they are asked to imagine a much happier scene in which the pen/dog is happy to run free. They could begin by listing words they would normally associate with a dog running around happily: for example, *pant, play, run, rush, scamper*.	**All Writing AFs, especially:** **Writing AF1** Write imaginative, interesting and thoughtful texts **Writing AF2** Produce texts which are appropriate to task, reader and purpose **Writing AF7** Select appropriate and effective vocabulary	195 196 197

Year 5 Poetry Unit 2 – Classic narrative poetry

Activity name	Strand and learning objectives	Notes on the activities	Assessment Focus	Page number
Soap opera challenge: 1, 2 and 3	**3. Group discussion and interaction** Plan and manage a group task over time using different levels of planning	**Soap opera challenge: 1, 2 and 3** should be carried out over a number of lessons. It links with text-level work on audience, character, plot and setting. Make enough copies of 'Soap opera challenge: 1 and 2' for the children to refer to, and make one copy of 'Soap opera challenge: 3' per group. To introduce the activity, ask the children about soap operas they have seen on the television, discussing what happens in them and what makes them different from other kinds of programmes or stories. Make it clear how long the children have to complete the challenge. The first stage of planning is to decide how to carry out the challenge, allocating responsibilities to different group members. For the initial discussions the children should appoint a chairperson (to keep order and make sure everyone has their say) and a scribe (to ensure important points are noted down). Check that the children's ideas are not copied directly from established soap operas. Also ensure that each group nominates a pair of 'directors' who will oversee the work of the whole group and ensure that everyone's work fits together as a whole. **Soap opera challenge: 2** provides a framework for recording decisions about the soap opera characters. The completed sheet could be photocopied for each pair in the group, so that they can refer to it as they carry out subsequent tasks. **Soap opera challenge: 3** helps the children to carry out the paired tasks A, B and C. The children will need to come together as a group again to act out the trailer. Once the challenge has been completed, the groups should present their work to the class. Encourage each group to assess how well they organised the challenge.	**Speaking and listening AF2** Listen and respond to others, including in pairs and groups, shaping meanings through suggestions, comments, and question	198–200
How well did your group do?	**3. Group discussion and interaction** Understand different ways to take the lead and support others in groups	**How well did your group do?** is a simple assessment sheet that can be used with the children after a group discussion. The features of 'good discussion' can be highlighted before a discussion session to introduce them or to remind the children of them. This page also helps the children to recognise how a discussion helped them to complete a task successfully. **Vocabulary:** *lead, plan, role, support, task*.	**Speaking and listening AF2** Listen and respond to others, including in pairs and groups, shaping meanings through suggestions, comments, and question	201

Section	Objective	Teaching notes	Assessment focus	Page
Aladdin playscript Aladdin characters Model theatre	**4. Drama** Use and recognise the impact of theatrical effects in drama	**Aladdin playscript, Aladdin characters** and **Model theatre** focus on theatrical effects and their impact. The children write a playscript and then perform it in a model theatre. You may need to draw attention to the difference between acting a performance in class and putting on a performance in a model theatre. Explain that the children may choose any episode in the Aladdin story. Once the scenes have been written and practised, allow opportunities for the groups to perform their scenes to the class, and invite comments from the audience on how effective each performance was. **How to make the model theatre:** 1) Colour and cut out the theatre scenery. 2) Turn an empty shoe box upside down. 3) Glue the theatre scenery onto the base of the box. 4) Cut out the stage area from the box. 5) Cut holes in the side panels of the box so that the characters can be inserted.	**Speaking and listening AF4** Understand the range and uses of spoken language, commenting on meaning and impact and draw on this when talking to others	202–204
Weird words	**6. Word structure and spelling** Spell words containing unstressed vowels	**Weird words** helps the children to develop a strategy for reading and spelling difficult words through noticing and describing their important features. After they have completed the activity you could read out the words for them to try to spell (provide a copy of the page, edited using the CD-ROM, with the words deleted from the word-bank). They could also choose a word that they often spell wrongly and write a 'weird word' description of it. Tell them to focus on the unusual or tricky part of the word in their description.	**Writing AF8** Use correct spelling	205
Words of a feather	**6. Word structure and spelling** Group and classify words according to their spelling patterns and their meanings	**Words of a feather** focuses on grouping and classifying words by their meanings. These pages could be edited using the CD-ROM. Possible answers for page 206: *dementia, mental, mentality, sentiment; account, count, miscount, recount; historian, historic, story; real, realist, reality, readly; unreal; spark, sparkler, sparkling; sensation, sense, sensitive, sensor; innovate, novel, novelty; optic, optics, optician; mass, massed, massive.* Other useful words: *luminous, revolve, deserve, resist, direct.*	**Writing AF8** Use correct spelling	206
	7. Understanding and interpreting texts Make notes on and use evidence from across a text to explain events or ideas		**Reading AF2** Understand, describe, select or retrieve information, events or ideas from texts and use quotation and reference to text **Reading AF3** Deduce, infer or interpret information, events or ideas from texts **Reading AF1** Use a range of strategies including accurate decoding of text, to read for meaning **Reading AF4** Identify and comment on the structure and organisation of texts, including grammatical and presentational features at text level **Reading AF5** Explain and comment on writers' uses of language, including grammatical and literary features at word and sentence level	
Is there anybody there? The traveller The Listeners The Listeners atmosphere	**7. Understanding and interpreting texts** Explore how writers use language for comic and dramatic effects	**Is there anybody there?** and **The traveller** prepare for the introduction of the poem *The Listeners* by Walter de la Mare (page 209). The first image (page 209) provides a focus for exploring the setting and its atmosphere and predicting what might happen there before the children read the poem. The second activity (page 210) introduces the character (the traveller) and prepares the children for what happens in the poem, which presents a short episode from a story, leaving the reader with a mystery. You could also prepare a 'story bag' containing objects linked with the poem for the children to explore and discuss: a riding whip, stirrups, reins, boots, an envelope sealed with sealing wax bearing an illegible (perhaps water-smudged) name written in pen and ink, a cloth or leather pouch or bag, a picture of a horse, a horse-shoe. **The Listeners** presents the poem *The Listeners* by Walter de la Mare. After introducing the poem (pages 208–210), read it to the children and allow them time to read it again for themselves and talk to their groups about it. Ask them why the traveller might be knocking at the door, who might be in the house (if anyone) and why no one was there if the traveller had said he would come. Also ask them what they think might happen next. Page 210 could be used for group work at this point. Re-read the first four lines with them, highlighting the use of language to communicate the look and atmosphere of the setting. Then read the next four lines and ask the children about the contrast (the knocking on the door in the silence of the wooded setting). **The Listeners atmosphere** focuses on the atmosphere of the poem. This could be used alongside page 209, after the children have read the poem but before they have identified the words that create the atmosphere. Before they begin to sort these cards they could write some of their own ideas about the atmosphere of the poem and write words on other cards (provide a blank copy of the grid).	**Reading AF2** Understand, describe, select or retrieve information, events or ideas from texts and use quotation and reference to text **Reading AF3** Deduce, infer or interpret information, events or ideas from texts **Reading AF1** Use a range of strategies including accurate decoding of text, to read for meaning **Reading AF4** Identify and comment on the structure and organisation of texts, including grammatical and presentational features at text level **Reading AF5** Explain and comment on writers' uses of language, including grammatical and literary features at word and sentence level	207–208 209 210

Year 5 Poetry Unit 3 – Choral and performance

Activity name	Strand and learning objectives	Notes on the activities	Assessment Focus	Page number
Listening to poems	**4. Drama** Use and recognise the impact of theatrical effects in drama	**Listening to poems** provides a format to help the children to record their responses to poems they listen to. These could be on the radio, television, CD-ROMs, DVDs or the Internet but the children will not see the texts before they hear them. It is useful to prepare for this by discussing a poem they listen to and using it to demonstrate the meanings of pace, rhythm, mood, meaning and message. Otherwise use CDs or online recordings. Discuss the fact that some poetry is part of an oral tradition and that books and printing have changed the way we encounter poetry (in modern UK culture at least).		211
Read it aloud		**Read it aloud** is about how to read a poem. In this activity the children read a poem they have not listened to and discuss the best ways of reading it. They should first consider what the poet is saying and then consider different tones of voice for reading different sections of the poem. The first stanza is a warning to the woman's friends and family, spoken with the defiance of a naughty child. The second stanza continues in this vein but the third provides contrast by describing the real lifestyle of the woman and should be spoken in a prim and proper way. Then the fourth stanza introduces a touch of mischief, as if the woman is about to try out some of her ideas.		212
Sounds good	**7. Understanding and interpreting texts** Explore how writers use language for comic and dramatic effects	**Sounds good** presents a poem that creates an image of stillness and calm while saying that there is no time for this; it creates an image of what could be and as such is a good example of persuasive writing. Through contrast, it seems to say 'This is what we should be doing'. The children are asked to identify the words and phrases and the poetic devices that help to create this atmosphere: the rhyme of long vowel sounds (and their repetition) in words such as *care, stare, boughs, cows, pass, grass, light, night, glance, dance;* and alliteration of soft consonants and the slow pace they create in words such as *life, if, stand, stare, streams, stars.*	**Reading AF2** Understand, describe, select or retrieve information, events or ideas from texts and use quotation and reference to text **Reading AF3** Deduce, infer or interpret information, events or ideas from texts **Reading AF1** Use a range of strategies including accurate decoding of text, to read for meaning **Reading AF4** Identify and comment on the structure and organisation of texts, including grammatical and presentational features at text level **Reading AF5** Explain and comment on writers' uses of language, including grammatical and literary features at word and sentence level	213
Sounds good to me	**8. Engaging with and responding to texts** Compare the usefulness of techniques such as visualisation, prediction, empathy, in exploring the meaning of texts	**Sounds good to me** helps the children to record their responses to the poems they most like listening to. They identify the words and phrases whose sounds they enjoy and which create effects such as fear, excitement, stillness, humour. Children could also record themselves and others performing their favourite poems to create a class poetry anthology.	**All Reading AFs, especially:** **Reading AF6** Identify and comment on writers' purposes and viewpoints and the overall effect of the text on the reader **Reading AF3** Deduce, infer or interpret information, events or ideas from texts **Reading AF7** Relate texts to their social, cultural and historical contexts and literary traditions	214
Performance evaluator	**9. Creating and shaping texts** Reflect independently and critically on their own writing and edit and improve it	**Performance evaluator** provides support to help the children to reflect independently and critically on their own writing or that of others and on the performance itself, thus providing a useful speaking and listening activity.	**All Writing AFs, especially:** **Writing AF1** Write imaginative, interesting and thoughtful texts **Writing AF2** Produce texts which are appropriate to task, reader and purpose **Writing AF7** Select appropriate and effective vocabulary	215
Performance poet	**9. Creating and shaping texts** Adapt non-narrative forms and styles to write fiction or factual texts, including poems	**Performance poet** provides a planning format to help the children to adapt a poem to write their own poem for performance, using language to create effects such as humour, excitement and so on. They also consider the structure of the poem: rhyme pattern, length of lines and rhythm. Remind the children that the poem will be written so that it can be performed. Can they tell you the characteristics of performance poems? They should draw on their knowledge of poems. They can then rehearse, perform, share, evaluate and improve their poems.	**All Writing AFs, especially:** **Writing AF1** Write imaginative, interesting and thoughtful texts **Writing AF2** Produce texts which are appropriate to task, reader and purpose **Writing AF7** Select appropriate and effective vocabulary	216

Competition: 1

- **Think about a competition you could hold in your school. It should:**

Work in a group.

★ be safe

★ interest as many children as possible

★ be fair to children of different ages

- **Make a note of every idea without discussing it.**

Our ideas

- **Discuss the advantages of each idea, then make a shortlist of three.**
- **List their advantages and disadvantages.**
- **Choose the most promising one.**

The group must agree on the choice.

Idea	Advantages	Disadvantages

NOW TRY THIS!

- **Choose a reporter to present your idea to the class.**
- **Help the reporter to think of ways of persuading the class.**

Teachers' note Ask the children to talk together about the kinds of competition they enjoy and to come up with ideas for a whole-school competition. They should first list all their ideas without comment, then take each idea in turn and decide whether it would interest as many children as possible and how feasible it might be in terms of practicality, organisation, time and expense.

A Lesson for Every Day
Literacy
9-10 Years
© A&C Black

27

Competition: 2

- **Plan a competition.**
- **Each group will present its plan to the class.**
- **The class can choose the plan that will work the best.**

Your group needs:

| a leader | a mentor | a scribe | a reporter |

Work in a group.

Competition description _____

How to enter the competition

How we shall organise the competition

The winner will be the person who _____

Rules

NOW TRY THIS!

- **Help the reporter to plan a talk about your plan.**

Teachers' note The children should first have completed 'Competition: 1'. Each group should have agreed on a competition they would like to run at school. They could then elect a spokesperson to speak to the class about their idea and the class could discuss this and take a vote.

A Lesson for Every Day
Literacy
9-10 Years
© A&C Black

Group leader

- ● **What should a group leader do?**
- ● **Choose the cards that give the six most important actions.**
- ● **Then share your ideas with your group.**

Tell group members what to do.	Ask group members what they think.	Tell group members that they must say something.
Ask group members to explain their views.	Tell group members when to stop speaking.	Encourage quiet members to speak.
Decide what the group should do.	Explain a task to the group.	Remind the group about timing.
Stop group members talking about other topics than the task they are meant to do.	Remind the group about the task, if necessary.	Decide who will speak and when.
Write notes about what the group decides to do.	Present the group's work to the class.	Tell group members to be quiet if they say too much.
Check that the group members agree about any decisions.	Tell the group that they must do as you say while you are the leader.	Make sure the group behaves well.

Teachers' note The children should think about how to lead a group and choose the six most important actions. Ask them how they will justify their choices; the group can then discuss them and make an agreed choice of six actions. To share their ideas with other groups, each group could elect someone to visit other groups and make a note of their lists.

A Lesson for Every Day
Literacy
9–10 Years
© A&C Black

29

Sort it out!

- **Read about this family argument**

The Kellys live in a three-bedroom house. The largest bedroom is shared by Lisa (aged 21) and Sarah (aged 10). Mr and Mrs Kelly have the second largest bedroom. Nicola (aged 18) has the smallest.

Lisa is about to move out and Sarah wants the largest bedroom all to herself. 'It's always been my room,' she says, 'and I've never had a room of my own.'

But Nicola wants the big bedroom, too. 'I'm older,' she argues. 'I need a room big enough to do my college work and have my friends round.'

The quarrel gets worse when Mrs Kelly pipes up, 'What about us? Shouldn't we have the largest room?'

- **Work in a group of four. Each person should take care of one of these roles:** | Sarah | Nicola | Mrs Kelly | Chairperson |

- **Discuss the problem in role.**

- **Every five minutes, change roles. Everyone should have a turn at being the chairperson.**

- **At the end of the discussion, colour the stars to show how well you did.**

| ★☆☆☆☆ = I need to practise this. | ★★★★★ = I did this well. |

When I was chairperson:

I led the discussion effectively.	☆☆☆☆☆
I made sure everyone had a chance to speak.	☆☆☆☆☆
I listened carefully to what others said.	☆☆☆☆☆
I responded in an appropriate way.	☆☆☆☆☆

NOW TRY THIS!

- **Discuss with your group how well you took the lead. What have you learned about being a good chairperson?**

Teachers' note Give each child a copy of this page. First discuss that the role of the chairperson is to manage the discussion, listening to others and making sure everyone has their say. Explain that this situation does not have a 'right answer', and all viewpoints should be considered by the group.

A Lesson for Every Day
Literacy
9–10 Years
© A&C Black

Deciding

- Think about a discussion you have had with your group.
- What did you do at each stage?
- Write on the flow-chart.

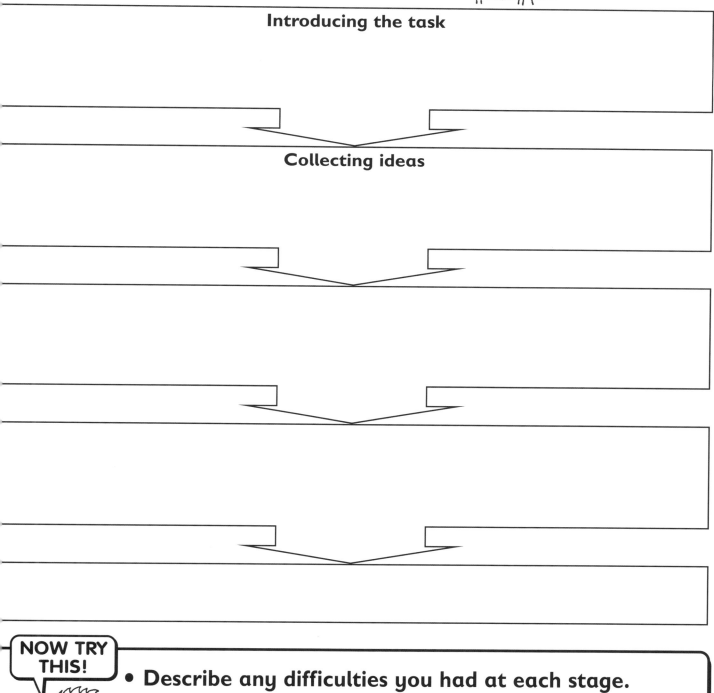

Introducing the task

Collecting ideas

NOW TRY THIS!

- Describe any difficulties you had at each stage.

achers' note The children might need help in identifying the stages of a discussion they have had nd might not need to use every section of the flow-chart): other stages include discussing their ideas, llecting facts, asking questions, making choices or decisions, recording their choices or decisions d reporting them to the class or to other groups.

A Lesson for Every Day
Literacy
9–10 Years
© A&C Black

The fear factor

Work in a group.

- **Read the letter. Try to agree which word is best for each space.**

The words should help to show how scary the flight was

> Dear Wayne,
>
> The flight was [＿＿＿＿＿].
> I saw a corkscrew shaped like a tornado
>
> and heard a [＿＿＿＿＿] noise.
>
> The plane suddenly [＿＿＿＿＿]
> up about 100 metres and then
>
> [＿＿＿＿＿] down again.
>
> Everything began to [＿＿＿＿＿].
>
> Mum was [＿＿＿＿＿].
>
> Children were [＿＿＿＿＿].
>
> I cried with [＿＿＿＿＿] when
> we finally landed. We have had storms,
> wind and rain for two days.
>
> Love Amy
>
> xxx

horrible
unpleasant
scary

deafening
roaring
whirring

lifted
shot
whooshed

dropped
fell
plunged

rattle
shake
tremble

frightened
speechless
terrified

crying
screaming
sobbing

happiness
joy
relief

NOW TRY THIS!

- **Join with another group. Talk to them about how you agreed which word to choose. Did eveyone have their say? Did you have to take a vote?**

Teachers' note Split the class into groups of four and give each group a copy of this page. Explain to the children that there is no 'correct answer', but that it is important to give reasons why certain words are better than others in a particular context. They should try to ensure that everyone in the group has their say. They may have to vote to reach a decision.

A Lesson for Every Day
Literacy
9–10 Years
© A&C Black

32

Anne Fine story openings

- **Read these story openings.**
- **Then fill in the spaces on page 34.**

A Really Awful Start

When Bill Simpson woke up on Monday morning, he found he was a girl.

He was still standing staring at himself in the mirror, quite baffled, when his mother swept in.

"Why don't you wear this pretty pink dress?" she said.

"I never wear dresses," Bill burst out.

"I know," his mother said. "It's such a pity.'

And, to his astonishment, before he could even begin to argue, she had dropped the dress over his head and zipped up the back.

"I'll leave you to do up the shell buttons," she said. "They're a bit fiddly and I'm late for work."

And she swept out, leaving him staring in dismay at the mirror. In it, a girl with his curly red hair and wearing a pretty pink frock with fiddly shell buttons was staring back at him in equal dismay.

From *Bill's New Frock* by Anne Fine

Bad News Bear

I'm not a total lame-brain. Nor am I intergalactically stupid. And I don't go wimp-eyed and soggy-nosed when bad things happen to me. But I confess, as I looked round the dismal swamp that was to be my new classroom, I did feel a little bit cheesy. Oh, yes. I was one definite Bad News Bear.

"Lovely news, everyone!"

Miss Tate clapped her hands and turned to the lines of dim-bulbs staring at me over their grubby little desks.

"We have somebody new this term," she said. "Isn't that nice?" She beamed. "And here he is. He's just flown in from America and his name is Howard Chester."

"Chester Howard," I corrected her.

But she wasn't listening. She was busy craning round the room, searching for a spare desk. And I couldn't be bothered to say it again. I reckoned she was probably bright enough to pick it up in time. So I just carried my stuff over to the empty desk she was pointing towards, in the back row.

"And that's Joe Gardener beside you," Miss Tate cooed after me.

"Hi, Gardener Joe," I muttered, as I sat down.

From *How to Write Really Badly* by Anne Fine

Story openings

- What is the author trying to do in the [opening]?
- Write notes about how she does this.

Title _____ Author _____

Set the scene	Introduce main character
Detailed description? Recount? Dialogue?	Character as narrator? Author as narrator? Dialogue? Description?
Grab reader's interest	**Introduce relationships**
Action? Problem? Interesting point of view? Mystery?	Family? Friends? Teacher/pupils? Tension or struggle?

NOW TRY THIS!

- Compare the openings of four books by the same author.
- List the similarities and differences.

Teachers' note Use this with 'Anne Fine story openings' or a different author. Ask the children how the author uses the opening: how she introduces the characters, the setting and the story. If this sheet is used for a story by a male author change the bullet point in the instructions to 'he'.

A Lesson for Every Day
Literacy
9-10 Years
© A&C Black

A Martian comes to stay

Read the passage.

Then fill in the chart on 'Stories by Penelope Lively'.

It was on the second day of Peter's holiday with his grandmother that the Martian came to the cottage. There was a knock at the door and when he went to open it there was this small green person with webbed feet and eyes on the end of stumpy antennae who said, perfectly politely, "I wonder if I might bother you for the loan of a spanner?"

"Sure," said Peter. "I'll ask my gran."

Gran was in the back garden, it being a nice sunny day. Peter said, "There's a Martian at the door who'd like to borrow a spanner."

Gran looked at him over her knitting. "Is there, dear? Have a look in Grandad's toolbox, there should be one there."

Peter found the spanner and took it back to the Martian, who held out a rather oddly-constructed hand and thanked him warmly. "We've got some trouble with the gears or something and had to make an emergency landing. And now the mechanic says he left his tools back at base. I ask you! It's all a mystery to me – I'm just the steward. Anyway – thanks a lot. I'll bring it back in a minute." And he padded away up the lane. There was no one around, but then there wasn't likely to be: the cottage was a quarter of a mile from the village and hardly anyone came by except the occasional farm tractor and the odd holidaymaker who'd got lost. Peter went back into the garden.

"Should have offered him a cup of tea," said Gran. "He'll have had a fair journey, I shouldn't wonder."

"Yes," said Peter. "I didn't think of that."

In precisely three minutes' time there was another knock at the door. The Martian was there, looking distinctly agitated. He said, "They've gone."

"Who's gone?" said Peter.

"The others. The spaceship. All of them. They've taken off and left me."

Gran by now had come through from the garden. She hitched her specs up her nose and looked down at the Martian, who was about three and a half feet high. "You'd best come in," she said, "while we have a think. Gone, you say? Where was it, this thing of yours?"

From *A Martian Comes to Stay* by Penelope Lively

teachers' note Read the passage with the children or give them time to read it independently. Ask them if it made them want to read the rest of the story. Ask for reasons. What did they not like? What made them want to read more? Discuss how Penelope Lively engages the reader's interest. See also 'Stories by Penelope Lively' on page 36.

A Lesson for Every Day
Literacy
9–10 Years
© A&C Black

Stories by Penelope Lively

- Read the passage with a friend.
- Compare it with other stories by Penelope Lively.
- Write notes on the chart.

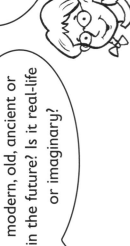

Is it an adventure, mystery, suspense story, myth, legend, historical story or science fiction?

Is it modern, nearly modern, old, ancient or in the future? Is it real-life or imaginary?

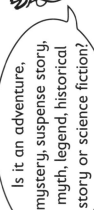

Are they ordinary everyday characters? Do they meet fantastical ones? Think about their relationships.

Title	Type of story	Setting	Characters
A Martian comes to stay			

NOW TRY THIS!

- Make another chart to compare themes or issues from one author's stories.

| friendship | prejudice | other theme or issue |

Teachers' note Use this with 'A martian comes to stay'. Ask the children to consider the different types of story they know and in which categories this one could fit. Is it a realistic or imaginary setting? Are the characters realistic or imaginary? Compare it with other stories by Penelope Lively and note the main similarities.

A Lesson for Every Day
Literacy
9–10 Years
© A&C Black

Open a story

Use the story opening **as a model for your own story about finding something.**

Think about ...   ... what is found ...   ... where ...   ... who finds it.

It was Kirstie who found it. It was lying just above the high-tide mark, a squarish package-shaped object, the colour of seaweed, with a long tendril sticking out from each of its four corners.

It was exactly the shape, in fact, of the 'mermaids' purses', the little horny egg capsules of the dogfish, that were commonly washed up on the beach. But this one was the size of a large biscuit tin!

'Look what I've found!' shouted Kirstie. 'Quick, come and look!'

From *The Water Horse* by Dick King-Smith

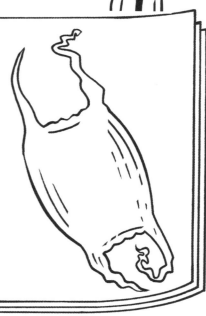

Your story

Title _____

was _____ who found it. It was _____

_____

_____

_____

_____

_____

NOW TRY THIS!

- **What happened next?**
- **Plan the story.**

achers' note Ask the children how the opening invites the reader to read on. What questions does aise? (for example, What did Kirstie find? Where? What is special about it?) You could also discuss w the writer tells readers what a mermaid's purse is and describes it. Ask the children to imagine ir story character finding something special – on a beach or in another setting.

Start with a question

- **Write a story** opening **that starts with a** question **.**
- **Introduce the main** characters **.**
- **Describe the** setting **.**
- **Recount the first event of the story.**

'What's that noise?' said Mrs Hogget, sticking her comfortable round red face out of the kitchen window. 'Listen, there 'tis again, did you hear it, what a racket, what a row, anybody'd think someone was being murdered, oh dearie me, whatever is it, just listen to it, will you?'

Farmer Hogget listened. From the usually quiet valley below the farm came a medley of sounds: the oompah oompah of a brass band, the shouts of children, the rattle and thump of a skittle alley, and every now and then a very high, very loud, very angry-sounding squealing lasting perhaps seconds.

Farmer Hogget pulled out an old pocket-watch as big round as a saucer and looked at it. 'Fair starts at two,' he said. 'It's started.'

'I knows that,' said Mrs Hogget, 'because I'm late now with all these cakes and jams, pickles and preserves as is meant to be on the Produce Stall this very minute, and, who's going to take them there, I'd like to know, why you are, but afore you does, what's that noise?'

The squealing sounded again.

From *The Sheep-pig* by Dick King-Smith

'_____ ,' asked _____

_____

_____

_____

_____

_____

_____

_____

_____

Who asked the question?

Describe the character.

Where is this? What was going on in the background?

What did the other character say and do?

NOW TRY THIS!

- **Continue the** dialogue **of your story.**

Teachers' note Ask the children how the opening invites the reader to read on. What do they want to know? Give them time to imagine another setting in which someone hears (or smells) something and then ask them to model their story opening on the passage – starting with a question and then gradually revealing what is happening.

A Lesson for Every Day
Literacy
9–10 Years
© A&C Black

The temptation: 1

The author describes only the important features of the setting .
- Underline these.
- In a different colour, underline the words that show William's thoughts.
- Predict what happens next.
- Write notes about this.

Suddenly his eye lit on the notice: "To stop the train, pull down the chain."

William stretched out his hand to it, then read: "Penalty for improper use, £5", and, after a hasty mental calculation that assessed his entire capital at the sum of one shilling and sixpence halfpenny, put his hand down again.

But the fascination of it was more than he could resist. He fingered the chain, and imagined himself pulling it. He wondered if it really worked and, if it worked, how it worked. It probably put on a sort of brake. There wouldn't be any harm in just pulling it a tiny bit. That would only just make the train go a little bit more slowly. No one would even notice it.

He pulled the chain an infinitesimal fraction.

Nothing happened.

He pulled it a little harder.

Still nothing happened.

He pulled it harder still. There was a sudden screaming of brakes, and the train drew to an abrupt standstill. William crouched in his corner of the carriage, frozen with horror. Perhaps, he thought desperately, if he sat quite still and didn't move or breathe, they wouldn't know who'd done it.

From *Sweet William* by Richmal Crompton

NOW TRY THIS!

- Continue the scene.
- Write William's thoughts.
- Write what William and any other characters said and did.

Teachers' note Ask the children how they felt when reading the passage. Did they want William to pull the communication cord? Did they guess what he would do? Ask them to notice how the author builds up the feeling of tension by recounting William's thoughts and his tentative reaching towards the cord, having second thoughts, then wondering if just a little pull would have just a little effect.

A Lesson for Every Day
Literacy
9-10 Years
© A&C Black

The temptation: 2

- **Write your own 'temptation' story** $\boxed{\text{chapter}}$.
- **Use the passage from *Sweet William* as a model.**

Chapter plan

Character _____

_____

Setting _____

_____

Temptation _____

_____

What the character does _____

_____

_____

_____

_____

_____

_____

_____

_____

_____

_____

_____

_____

_____

_____

_____

What does the character notice?

Write a paragraph. Give information about the character and setting.

What goes through the character's mind?

Write a paragraph about the character's discussion with himself or herself.

What does he or she do? What happens?

Continue on the back of the sheet if you need to.

NOW TRY THIS!

- **Write a chapter about the** $\boxed{\text{consequences}}$ **of the temptation.**

---

40 **Teachers' note** The children could first talk to a friend about a situation in which they were tempted to do something they knew they should not. They could write their thoughts in speech bubbles. What did they do? What happened – or what might have happened if they had given in to the temptation? Ask them to record these in direct speech to create a feeling of tension.

A Lesson for Every Day
Literacy
9–10 Years
© A&C Black

Borrow a character

- Plan a story about a [character] from a story you have read.

Character's name _____   Story/stories _____

Author _____

Opening
What is the character doing?
Where?
What does the reader need to know about any past events?

Something happens
What happens?
What problems does it cause?

Climax
What happens to build up the tension, mystery or excitement?

Resolution
What happens to solve the problem or mystery?

Ending
How are all the events in the story linked to one another? What happens to the main character and any others?

Think about what you know about the character.

NOW TRY THIS!

- Write the first [chapter] of your story.
- Give it to a friend to [edit].

Teachers' note Use this to develop a story about any fictional character the children like. They can use their knowledge of the character to help them to imagine what he or she might do in a particular situation. You could present them with a situation: for example, seeing someone robbed, finding something valuable or overhearing a conversation that makes him or her want to find out more.

A Lesson for Every Day
Literacy
9-10 Years
© A&C Black

Add a comma

- **Read the speech bubbles with a partner.**
- **Put in** commas **and read them again.**
- **Notice how the commas help.**

, comma

In the corner where the picture used to be was a red stain.

They had two cats a dog a parrot a guinea pig and three rabbits.

We searched high and low but we could not find Mum's keys.

It was a bright sunny day with no wind so we put up a tent.

The house was full of books but I never saw anyone reading them.

If a program will not close press Control and Alt then press and release Delete.

Rub the flour and butter stir in the sugar then mix in the beaten egg.

He kept kicking the ball against the wall smiling at his skill until he heard the tinkle of broken glass.

They found a jellyfish on the beach close to the high tide mark and wondered if it was alive.

The sun shone the birds sang the flowers swayed in the wind and the bees buzzed all around.

NOW TRY THIS!

- **Look through some books.**
- **Find six sentences with commas.**
- **Rewrite them without commas and read them aloud.**
What difference do the commas make?

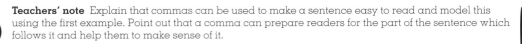

Teachers' note Explain that commas can be used to make a sentence easy to read and model this using the first example. Point out that a comma can prepare readers for the part of the sentence which follows it and help them to make sense of it.

A Lesson for Every Day
Literacy
9-10 Years
© A&C Black

Makes a change

Punctuation can change the meaning of a sentence.

- Change the punctuation to give each of these sentences a different meaning.

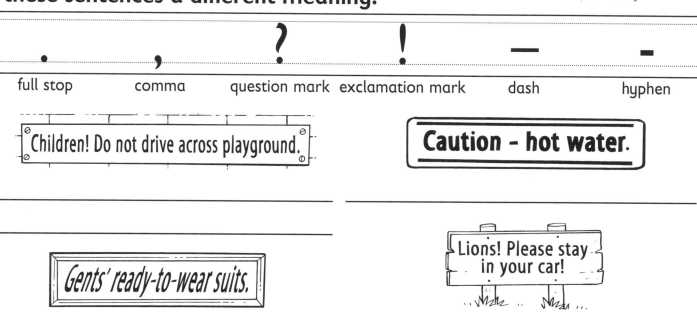

.	,	?	!	—	-
full stop	comma	question mark	exclamation mark	dash	hyphen

Children! Do not drive across playground.

Caution – hot water.

Gents' ready-to-wear suits.

Lions! Please stay in your car!

DON'T THROW-PEOPLE BELOW.

She was a pretty, tall girl.

 No-one knows me.

Call me 'Jim'.

 **NOW TRY THIS!**

- **Write the meanings of the sentences.**

Teachers' note Remind the children of their previous learning about commas and point out that punctuation marks can alter the meaning of a sentence. Model this by reading the examples in the picture aloud. Draw out that the wording in both is identical but that the punctuation makes the meanings different.

A Lesson for Every Day
Literacy
9-10 Years
© A&C Black

43

LIVERPOOL JOHN MOORES UNIVERSITY
LEARNING SERVICES

Conversation poem

- **Read the verses with a partner.**
- **Rewrite them as an ordinary** dialogue **– not as a poem. Use a separate sheet of paper.**
- **Miss out the** narrative .

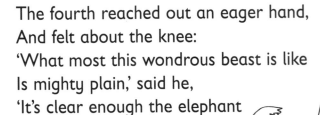

Think about layout, capital letters and punctuation.

From *The Six Blind Men and the Elephant*

The first approached the elephant,
And happening to fall
Against his broad and sturdy side,
At once began to bawl:
'God bless me! But the elephant
Is very like a wall!'

The second, feeling of the tusk,
Cried, 'Ho! what have we here
So very round and smooth and sharp?
To me it's mighty clear,
This wonder of an elephant
Is very like a spear!'

The third approached the animal,
And happening to take
The squirming trunk within his hands,
Thus boldly up and spake:
'I see,' said he, 'the elephant
Is very like a snake!'

The fourth reached out an eager hand,
And felt about the knee:
'What most this wondrous beast is like
Is mighty plain,' said he,
'It's clear enough the elephant
Is very like a tree!'

The fifth, who chanced to touch the ear,
Said, 'Even the blindest man
Can tell what this resembles most;
Deny the fact who can,
This marvel of an elephant
Is very like a fan!'

The sixth no sooner had begun
About the beast to grope,
Than, seizing on the swinging tail
That fell within his scope,
'I see,' said he, 'the elephant
Is very like a rope!'

John Godfrey Saxe

44

Teachers' note Remind the children about the punctuation and layout of dialogue, including starting a quotation from a new speaker on a new line and indenting it. Also remind them which words should begin with capital letters and about the punctuation of dialogue, including the positions of quotation marks and the punctuation at the end of the spoken words.

A Lesson for Every Day
Literacy
9–10 Years
© A&C Black

Story spidergram

- **Plan a story to tell to younger children.**
- **Draw lines to link the characters, objects and ideas.**
- **Write on the lines to show how these are linked in your story.**

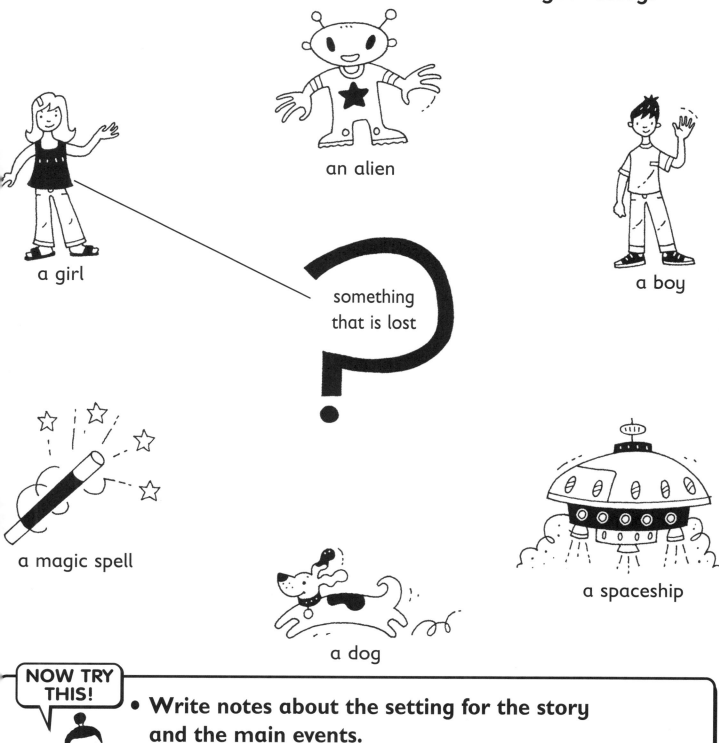

an alien

a girl

something that is lost

a boy

a magic spell

a dog

a spaceship

NOW TRY THIS!
- **Write notes about the setting for the story and the main events.**
- **Tell the story to a group.**

Teachers' note Give the children time to think about the story 'ingredients' and to come up with story ideas featuring some or all of them. They should draw lines to link them and write notes on. They should use this page as a prompt to help them to tell a story, rather than read aloud one they have written, enabling them to change it slightly each time.

A Lesson for Every Day
Literacy
9–10 Years
© A&C Black

The Three Little...

- **Plan your own version of *The Three Little Pigs* to tell to younger children.**
- **Choose some characters from the pictures.**
- **Make notes about:**

> Replace the pigs with different characters.

| homes the characters will make | who will attack them |

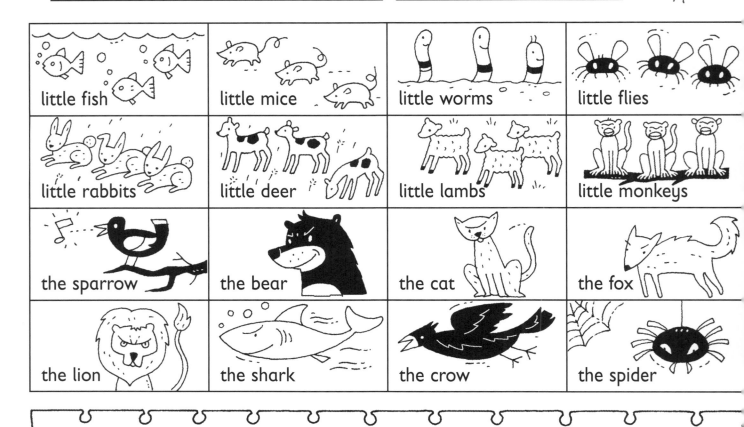

little fish	little mice	little worms	little flies
little rabbits	little deer	little lambs	little monkeys
the sparrow	the bear	the cat	the fox
the lion	the shark	the crow	the spider

_____

_____

_____

_____

NOW TRY THIS!

- **Share your story ideas with a friend.**
- **Practise telling it.**

Teachers' note The children should know the story of *The Three Little Pigs*. You could ask them to retell it to refresh their memories before they make up their own version based on a group of three characters plus another single character from this page.

A Lesson for Every Day
Literacy
9-10 Years
© A&C Black

Humpty Dumpty: 1

- **Make up your own story about Humpty Dumpty to tell to your class.**
- **Use recap to create humour.**

Humpty Dumpty sat on a wall
Was he pushed or did he fall?

Here are some ideas to get you started.

Scene of crime officer's notebook:

Incident: _large egg (male, age hard to establish) with serious head injuries._

Why were the army and cavalry called in?

NOW TRY THIS!

- **Continue the story using recap.**
- **Think of ways to make the story funny.**

Teachers' note Ask the children to imagine the scene as newspaper reporters and to write notes as if they are reporting a 'crime'. Read the questions on 'Humpty Dumpty: 2' with the children to help them clarify their thoughts and work through the egg-word list on 'Humpty Dumpty words' to help them express them. They could just write the story opening to get them started when they begin telling it.

A Lesson for Every Day
Literacy
9-10 Years
© A&C Black

47

Humpty Dumpty: 2

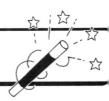

- **Answer these questions to help you to write your Humpty Dumpty story.**

Think about making the audience laugh.

Who found Humpty Dumpty?

What did they say when they called 999?

Who was arrested for pushing him off the wall?

How was this reported?

What did the army chiefs say about why the soldiers and horses were there?

NOW TRY THIS!

- **Make notes of useful words and phrases to use when you tell your story.**

Teachers' note Use this with page 'Humpty Dumpty: 1'. The children can use these questions to jog their memories about the original rhyme and to help them to create humour in their 'crime story'.

A Lesson for Every Day
Literacy
9-10 Years
© A&C Black

Humpty Dumpty words

This list contains words you could use in funny ways in your story.
Add a funny meaning and an example
of how each word might be used.
One has been started for you.

Think about puns.

Word	Funny meaning	Example
egg-couple	A pair of eggs, like a husband and wife.	
fry		
layer		
mother hen		
poacher		
scrambled		
soldiers		
hard-boiled		
soft-boiled		
sell by		

NOW TRY THIS!

• **Find ways of using some words from the egg-word list in your story.**

achers' note Use this with 'Humpty Dumpty: 1 and 2'. Encourage the children to use word-play in
eir humorous story. They are unlikely to use all these examples, but some children might be able
weave a considerable number of them into their stories and might even be able to come up with
hers of their own.

A Lesson for Every Day
Literacy
9-10 Years
© A&C Black

Negative questions

• What answers do the questioners want? Why?

Work with a partner.

Don't you think you deserve a special car?

Answer

Reason _____

_____

_____

Shouldn't you be in bed?

Answer

Reason _____

_____

_____

Can't you see I'm busy?

Answer

Reason _____

_____

_____

Wouldn't you like to have a nice relaxing holiday in the sunshine?

Answer

Reason _____

_____

_____

Don't you want us to have a nice garden?

Answer

Reason _____

_____

_____

Isn't it time you had a new carpet to match your lovely sofa?

Answer

Reason _____

_____

_____

NOW TRY THIS!

- **Turn the questions into positive questions.**
- **Make notes about how this affects the answers.**
- **Do they still serve the same purpose?**

Teachers' note Introduce the term negative question and use examples to model some (see *Notes on the activities*, page 8). Ask the children how these questions influence the answer and how the person being questioned might feel. You could also discuss who might ask negative questions, and why.

A Lesson for Every Day
Literacy
9–10 Years
© A&C Black

Negative to positive

Change the negative questions to make them positive.
Take turns to read a negative and positive pair to a partner.
Write your answers.
Say how you feel about being asked each question.

Complete this page with a partner.

Negative	Answer	Positive	Answer
Don't you think you should recycle your rubbish?			
Shouldn't you wash your hands before eating?			
Can't you understand what I'm saying?			
Have you never been on a plane?			

NOW TRY THIS!

- **Explain why you think each of these negative questions might be asked.**
- **Do you prefer answering negative or positive questions?**
- **Say why.**

Teachers' note The children should first have completed page 50. Ask them to read the negative question to a partner, who should answer; they then change the question, making it positive, and ask their partner this new question and write the answer. They then swap roles for the next question and so on.

A Lesson for Every Day
Literacy
9–10 Years
© A&C Black

How does it feel

- **Read about this situation.**

Jack is 10 and his brother Stephen is 13. Jack bought some chocolates from the local newsagent's to give to his mum on her birthday. On his way home he met a gang of older boys who stole the chocolates from him. One of the boys was his brother's friend, Paul.

Jack didn't have enough money to buy another box of chocolatess for his mum, so he went back to the newsagent's and stole one. His friend Chloe saw him do it.

- **Work in a group of four. Each of you take one of these roles.**

| Jack | | Jack's mum | | Shopkeeper | | Chloe |

- **Think about these questions. Then make notes about your character's point of view and feelings.**

Why did Jack think it was all right to steel another box of chocolates?

How would Jack's mum feel if she knew Jack had stolen the chocolates?

What could Jack have done instead?

Should Chloe tell anyone what she saw?

_____'s point of view	_____'s feelings

- **In role, discuss whether Jack had a good reason to do what he did.**

NOW TRY THIS!

- **In your group, talk about how your role-play helped you to understand the problem. Did you all agree on what Jack should have done?**

Teachers' note Give each child a copy of this page. Read the situation with the children and explain that they are going to use role-play to think about it from different points of view. During the plenary, discuss the issue of bullying and how to cope with it, with reference to what Jack could have done after the older boys stole from him.

A Lesson for Every Day
Literacy
9-10 Years
© A&C Black

The mad tea party

**Read the playscript of a scene from *Alice in Wonderland*
Work in a group of four. You are going to perform the
scene, using the stage directions to help you.
First decide who will play each character. Then talk about
how you will play the scene.**

What do the stage directions
tell you about the characters?

How will you
say the words?

How will you show how the
characters are feeling?

*Scene: a table set outside a house. The Hatter and the March Hare are having tea
at it. A Dormouse is sitting between them, fast asleep. Alice approaches.*

Hatter: No room! No room!
Alice *(indignantly)*: There's plenty of room! *(She
sits down in a big armchair at one end of the table.)*
March Hare *(waving his arm)*: Have some wine.
Alice *(looking around)*: I don't see any wine.
March Hare *(giggles to himself)*: There isn't any.
Alice *(angrily)*: Then it wasn't very civil of you to offer it.
March Hare: It wasn't very civil of you to sit down
without being invited.
Alice: I didn't know it was your table. It's laid for a
great many more than three. *(She sulks. There is silence.)*
Hatter *(staring at Alice with great curiosity)*: Your hair wants cutting.
Alice *(severely)*: You should learn not to make personal remarks. It's very rude.
Hatter *(opening his eyes very wide)*: Why is a raven like a writing desk?
Alice *(cheering up)*: Oh, I love riddles. I believe I can guess that.
March Hare: Do you mean that you think you can find out the answer to it?
Alice: Exactly so.
March Hare: Then you should say what you mean.
Alice *(hastily)*: I do. *(Pause.)* At least, I mean what I say – that's the same
thing, you know.
Hatter: Not the same thing a bit! You might just as well say that 'I see what
I eat' is the same thing as 'I eat what I see'!
Dormouse *(as though talking in his sleep)*: You might just as well say that 'I breathe when I
sleep' is the same thing as 'I sleep when I breathe'!
Hatter: It is the same thing with you. *(Silence)*

**NOW TRY
THIS!**

- **Discuss how you think the scene continues.**
- **Write the rest of the scene as a playscript.
Remember to use stage directions.**

achers' note Give each child a copy of this page and read the playscript to the children. Look at
amples of stage directions together and discuss what they tell us about the characters and how to
ge the play. For the extension activity, the children do not need to follow the actual events of *Alice
Wonderland*.

A Lesson for Every Day
Literacy
9–10 Years
© A&C Black

53

Unstressed vowels: 1

- **Circle the** unstressed vowel phoneme **in each word.**
- **Say the word to a friend in a way that helps you to remember how to spell the word.**
- **Write the word to show how you said it.**

Example:

NOW TRY THIS!

- **Investigate words with unstressed vowel phonemes.**
- **List the phonemes that are unstressed.**
- **Record these on a graph to show which occur most frequently.**

Teachers' note If necessary, introduce the term *unstressed vowel* to describe a vowel that is not spoken at all or sounds like *uh*. During the plenary session invite the children to say the words in a way that reminds them how to write the unstressed vowels.

A Lesson for Every Day
Literacy
9–10 Years
© A&C Black

Unstressed vowels: 2

- **Circle the** ⌐unstressed vowel phoneme⌐ **in each word.**
- **Say the word to a friend in a way that helps you to remember how to spell the word.**
- **Write the word to show how you said it.**

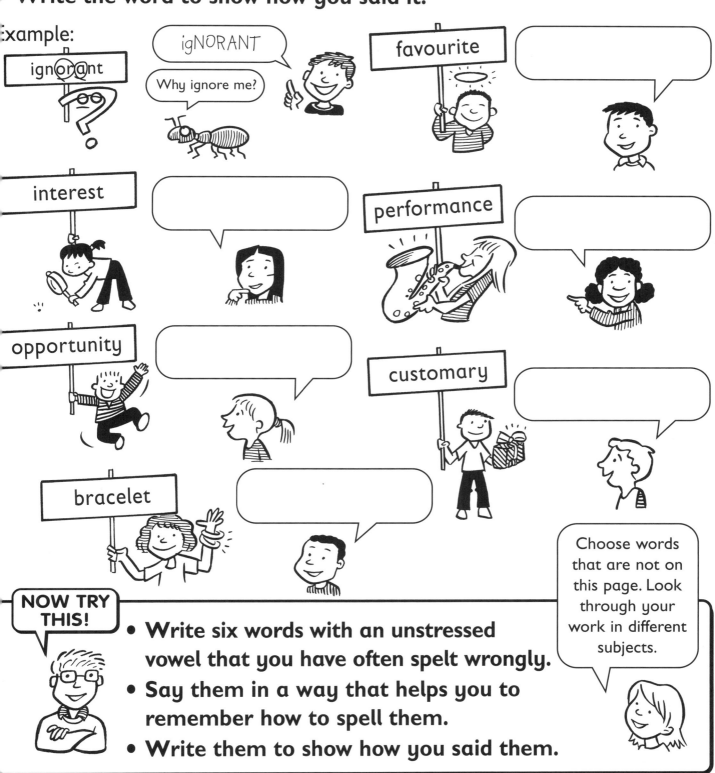

Example:

ignorant

igNORANT

Why ignore me?

favourite

interest

performance

opportunity

customary

bracelet

Choose words that are not on this page. Look through your work in different subjects.

NOW TRY THIS!

- **Write six words with an unstressed vowel that you have often spelt wrongly.**
- **Say them in a way that helps you to remember how to spell them.**
- **Write them to show how you said them.**

Teachers' note It helps if the children have first completed 'Unstressed vowels: 1'. During the plenary session the children could enact the 'mnemonic' spellings they have come up with.

A Lesson for Every Day
Literacy
9-10 Years
© A&C Black

Noun converter

- **Choose** suffixes **to convert the verbs and adjectives into nouns.**

Change the base words if necessary.

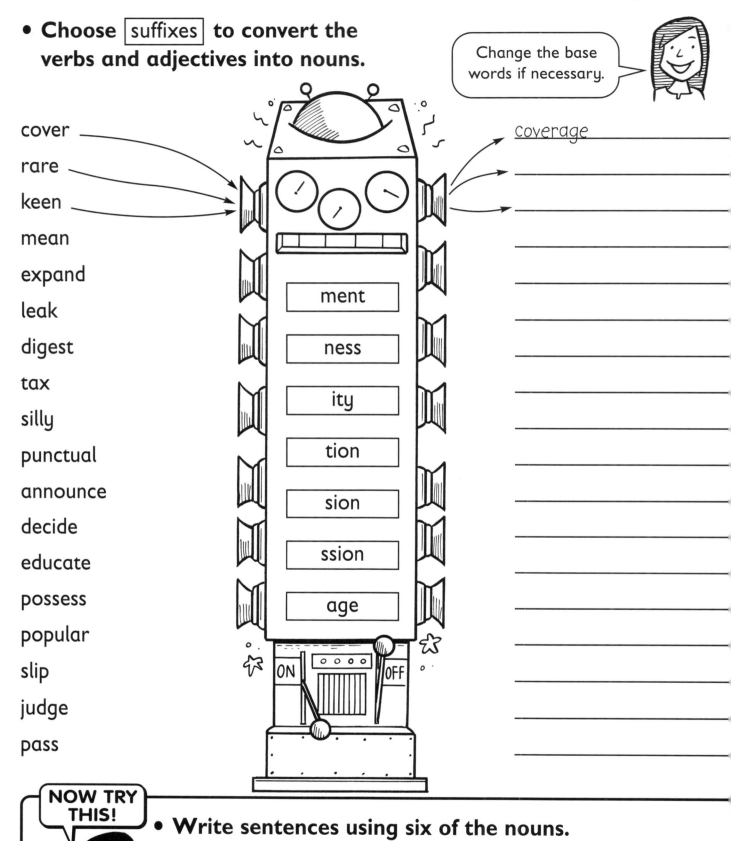

cover

rare

keen

mean

expand

leak

digest

tax

silly

punctual

announce

decide

educate

possess

popular

slip

judge

pass

ment

ness

ity

tion

sion

ssion

age

ON   OFF

coverage
_____

_____

_____

_____

_____

_____

_____

_____

_____

_____

_____

_____

_____

_____

_____

_____

_____

NOW TRY THIS!

- **Write sentences using six of the nouns.**

56 Teachers' note Ask the children for examples of nouns that are not objects: for example, *happiness,* *contentment, mission.* Point out the common noun suffixes -**ment**, -**ness**, -**ity**, -**tion**, -**sion** and -**age** and give a few examples with incorrect suffixes for them to correct: *sadment, visity, stopssion, ugliage.* Use examples to remind them how nouns, verbs and adjectives work in sentences.

A Lesson for Every Day
Literacy
9–10 Years
© A&C Black

What's my job?

- **Add the suffix** cian **to make words for the people.**

You might have to change the base word.

magic

_____

electrics

_____

mathematics

_____

politics

_____

beauty

_____

music

_____

diet

_____

technical

_____

optics

_____

NOW TRY THIS!

- **Compare** cian **words with** tion **words.**
- **What kinds of word have each suffix?**

  cian words are usually for _____

  tion words are usually for _____

eachers' note Remind the children of their previous learning about -**er** endings for people's jobs
eacher, writer and so on). Explain that the suffix -cian can also be used to make the name of a job.
uring the plenary session, ask them to describe how the base word changes before the suffix is
dded.

A Lesson for Every Day
Literacy
9-10 Years
© A&C Black

Noun suffixes

- Add a suffix to make another noun.
- Write a definition for the new noun.
- Does the base word change?
- Check your answers in a dictionary.

Base word	New noun	Definition
member	membership	Being a member
bored		
owner		
child		
baby		
leader		
citizen		
free		
adult		
partner		
wise		
parant		
scholar		
mother		
friend		
apprentice		

NOW TRY THIS!

- Use two different suffixes to make new nouns from king .
- Write the nouns and their definitions.

Teachers' note Ask the children to form a sentence using the first word in the chart and then to say what class of word *bored* is. Give them a sentence in which *bored* is used wrongly as a noun: for example, *The children complained of bored*. Explain how to convert this to a noun: *The children complained of boredom*. Remind them about abstract nouns (nouns for feelings, qualities and so on).

A Lesson for Every Day
Literacy
9–10 Years
© A&C Black

Fabulous fables

- **What is the message of each** fable ?
- **Write in the boxes.**

Work with
a friend.

The ant and the grasshopper

One summer's day a grasshopper was hopping about in a field, singing. An ant passed by carrying a huge ear of corn.

"Come and have fun instead of working," said the grasshopper.

"I am collecting food for the winter," said the ant. "You should do the same."

"Why bother about winter?" said the grasshopper. "We have plenty of food." The ant went on working. When the winter came the grasshopper starved, but the ants had plenty to eat.

The boy who cried wolf

There was once a shepherd boy who wanted some attention and excitement. One evening he rushed into the village shouting, "Wolf, wolf!" The villagers came running out to kill the wolf but they could not find it. The boy enjoyed this so much that a few days later he did it again. Again the villagers came to help. Again they found no wolf.

Not long afterwards a wolf began to attack the sheep. The boy ran to the village shouting, "Wolf, wolf!" This time no one came to help.

The fox and the crow

A crow perched in a tree holding a piece of meat. Before long a fox came along and wanted the meat. He said, "How beautiful the crow is! If her voice were as beautiful as her looks she would be queen of the birds." The crow wanted to show that her voice was beautiful, too, and opened her beak to caw. The meat fell to the ground. The fox snatched it up, and said to the crow, "Your voice is fine, but your brains are not."

The bundle of sticks

An old man who was dying asked his servant to bring a bundle of sticks, and he said to his eldest son, "Break it." The son strained and strained but, however hard he tried, he could not break the bundle. The other sons tried, too, but could not break it. "Untie the sticks and take one. Now, break it," said the father.

Each stick broke easily.

Teachers' note Ask the children what they know about fables (stories – usually very short – with a message). The best known fable-writers are Aesop (Greek, 6th century BCE) and Jean de la Fontaine (French, 17th century). After they have read the stories, invite feedback about messages, settings and characters (especially personification of animals).

A Lesson for Every Day
Literacy
9-10 Years
© **A&C Black**

Story sorts

- **Sort the stories into four sets.**
- **Think about the similarity between the stories in each set.**

Work with a friend.

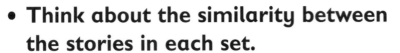

Persephone and the Pomegranate seeds	The Ant and the Grasshopper	Robin Hood and the Sheriff of Nottingham
The Lion and the Mouse	King Arthur and the Knights of the Round Table	Androcles and the Lion
The Three Little Pigs	King Alfred and the Burnt Cakes	King Midas (who turned everything he touched into gold)
The Gingerbread Man	The Hare and the Tortoise	The Story of the Glastonbury Thorn
Saint George and the Dragon	The Story of Rama and Sita	Goldilocks and the Three Bears
Jason and the Golden Fleece	The Minotaur	The Fox and the Hen

Teachers' note Recap the four categories with the children before starting. Ask the children to cut out the cards and, in groups, to identify the stories they (or some of them) know. Leave out any they do not know. Ask them to sort the cards into sets and to discuss how those in each set are similar. Invite feedback.

A Lesson for Every Day
Literacy
9–10 Years
© A&C Black

Creation myths

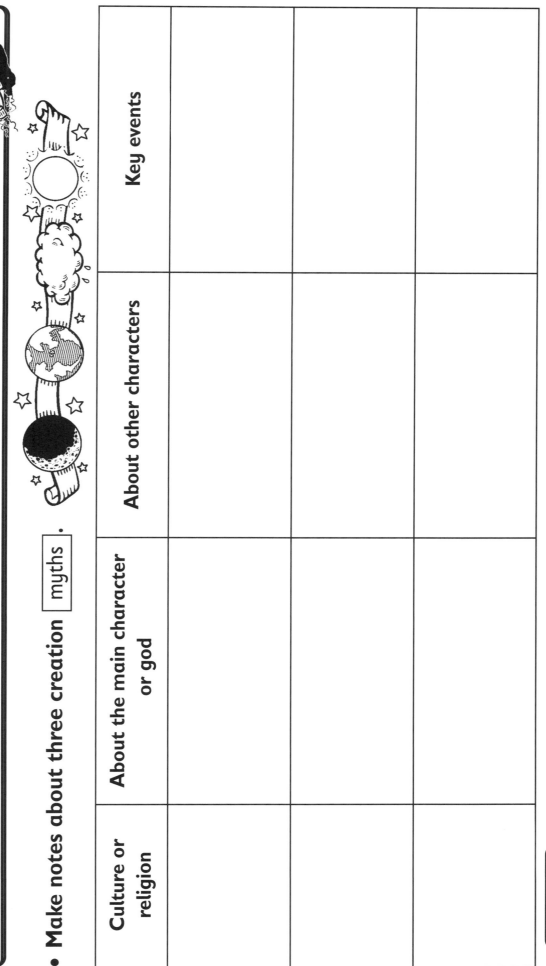

- Make notes about three creation myths .

Culture or religion	About the main character or god	About other characters	Key events

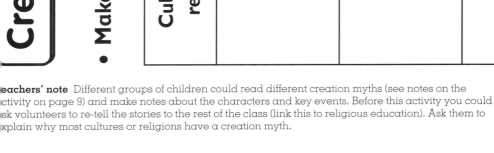

NOW TRY THIS!

- List the similarities between the creation myths.

A Lesson for Every Day
Literacy
9-10 Years
© **A&C Black**

Teachers' note Different groups of children could read different creation myths (see notes on the activity on page 9) and make notes about the characters and key events. Before this activity you could ask volunteers to re-tell the stories to the rest of the class (link this to religious education). Ask them to explain why most cultures or religions have a creation myth.

The rescue plan

Robin Hood and Will Scarlett are in the woods.

- **How can they rescue Maid Marian from the castle?**
- **Write** notes **about what might happen in each place.**

Dungeon

Mortimer's Hole

Curtain wall

Keep

Gatehouse

Woods

River Leen

62

Teachers' note The children first need to have read the legend of Robin Hood. It is also useful if they have looked at the software Castle Attack (see notes on page 10). They can then make notes about the problems Robin Hood and Will Scarlett might face as they try to rescue Maid Marian.

A Lesson for Every Day
Literacy
9–10 Years
© A&C Black

The rescue: game board

Opening

In two sentences, describe the historical setting. +2

In one sentence, say what happened before this story began. +1

Go back two. -1

Take a character card. Give three details about him or her. +3

Take a character card. Describe the character's personal qualities. +3

Go back six. -1

Take a settings card. Describe the setting. +3

Go back three. -1

+3

Take a settings card. Say why the setting is important.

Go back two. -1

Take a character card. Give three sentences about the character's life so far. +3

+2

Take a settings card. Describe the atmosphere here.

Go back three. -1

Go back one. -1

Take a character card. Describe a problem he or she faces. +2

+2 **Take a character card. Recount one action by this character.**

Describe the main problem faced by the key character. +3

Go back two. -1

Go back three. -1

Ending

Take a character card. Say how this character resolves a problem. +4

Take a settings card. Say how this place is important in resolving a problem. +4

Go back one. -1

Take a character card and a settings card. Say what important action the character does there. +4

achers' note The children should first have completed 'The rescue plan' on page 62. Use this with e cards on 'The rescue: game cards'. It is a game for four. Players place a counter on Opening and ke turns to roll a die to see how many squares to move. Different squares tell them to talk about parts the story setting or the characters. They must land on Ending to finish. They then plan a story based the settings and characters.

A Lesson for Every Day
Literacy
9-10 Years
© A&C Black

63

The rescue: game cards

Setting cards

A chapel in the castle wall

A dungeon

The gatehouse

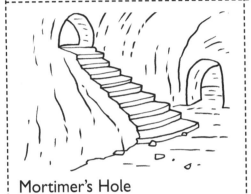

Mortimer's Hole

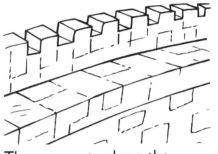

The ramparts along the curtain wall

The keep

Character cards

Robin Hood, a yeoman who became an outlaw and robbed the rich to help the poor

Maid Marian, a noblewoman and Robin's sweetheart

Will Scarlett, a kinsman of Robin Hood and his faithful supporter

Little John, Robin's right-hand man. A big man and a strong fighter

The Sheriff of Nottingham, who wanted Robin captured

Alan A'Dale, a minstrel and one of the outlaws

Teachers' note The children should first have completed 'The rescue plan'. Cut out the two sets of cards and place them face down in two piles. Use them with the game board on 'The rescue: game board'. Players pick up a setting or character card as directed. Once read, these are placed at the bottom of the pile. The children then plan a story based on the settings and characters. 'Legend research' will help.

A Lesson for Every Day
Literacy
9-10 Years
© A&C Black

Legend research

- Research the historical setting of a legend .
- **Find out about life at the time.**
- **Find out about key people and events of the time.**

The setting

Make notes about the place.

Life at the time

Real historical characters in the legend

Describe the characters. Note their important actions.

Time-line

Key events in the legend	Key events in history	Year

NOW TRY THIS!

- **Write an** introduction **to the legend.**
- **Read this aloud to interest the audience.**

Record the introduction.

Teachers' note This could be linked with work in history. The children could research a period they already know something about and then model their legend on the style of others they have read. Point out that authors always research the historical settings of their stories to help them to write accurately and make the stories convincing.

A Lesson for Every Day
Literacy
9–10 Years
© A&C Black

The hidden folk

- **Rewrite the story.**
- **Make it more interesting for the reader.**

Use direct speech.
Use connectives.
Describe some details.

The Hidden People
A folk-tale from Iceland

Once upon a time, God came to visit Adam and Eve. They received him with joy and showed him everything in their house. Then they showed him their children. God said they were very promising and full of hope. He asked Eve whether she had any other children. She said she had none.

But Eve had not finished washing the children and was ashamed to let God see any dirty, so she had hidden the unwashed ones. God knew this, of course, and said, "What humans hide from God, God will hide from humanity."

So the unwashed children became invisible. They went to live in mounds and hills. The elves are descended from them, but humans come from the children Eve had shown to God. Elves can only be seen by humans if the elves want to be seen.

What did the characters say? What did the children do?

How did Eve look?

Link how Eve looked to the other paragraphs. Use connectives. Describe where the elves live. Address the last sentence to the reader using 'you'.

_____

_____

_____

_____

_____

_____

_____

_____

Continue on the back of the sheet if you need

NOW TRY THIS!

- **Reread your version of the** | legend |.
- | Edit | **it and see if you can improve it.**

Teachers' note Read the folk-tale to the children and ask them if they enjoyed it. Discuss what would make it more interesting and enjoyable for the reader. Model how to improve the first three or four sentences (see Notes on the activities, page 10). Remind them of the rules for writing direct and reported speech.

A Lesson for Every Day
Literacy
9–10 Years
© A&C Black

Storyteller

Read these sentences from a story. Rewrite them for a reader aged five to six.

You could split the sentences into shorter ones. You could miss some out.

You could use different words.

Once upon a time there was a stick of wood. It was not a fine stick, either, but just such another as you would put in the fireplace to heat the room.

I do not know how it came about, but one fine day this stick of wood was found in the carpenter's shop of an old man named Antonio. Everybody called him Master Cherry, however, because of the colour of his nose, which was red and shiny like a ripe cherry.

As soon as Master Cherry saw the stick of wood he was delighted. He rubbed his hands together and mumbled to himself, "The very thing! This stick will make a fine table leg."

Saying this, he picked up a sharp axe to begin to smooth off the bark; but just as he was about to strike, he stopped with his arm in the air, for he thought he heard a thin sharp voice cry out, "Do not strike me too hard!"

From *Pinocchio* by Carlo Collodi

You could add a picture.   You could change the layout.

NOW TRY THIS!

- **Look at the changes you made for a younger reader.**
- **List the changes you made to the punctuation.**

Teachers' note Ask the children what they learned about how texts are made suitable for audiences of different ages. Ask them which age group they think this passage is for. Discuss how they would change it to make it suitable for younger children.

A Lesson for Every Day
Literacy
9–10 Years
© A&C Black

Recount to dialogue

- **Rewrite these sentences as** dialogue .

Use speech marks.

Change the punctuation where you need to.

Change or add words where you need to.

A story from the *Upanishads* (books of Hindu teaching)

Uddalaka asked Svetaketu if he had learned how to hear what cannot be heard, to see what cannot be seen, to know what cannot be known.

Svetaketu asked him what that was.

Uddalaka replied by asking him to cut open the fig he had and to tell him what he saw.

Svetaketu said that he saw tiny seeds.

Uddalaka told him to cut open a seed and tell him what he saw there.

Svetaketu said that he saw nothing.

Uddalaka said that the finest essence was in that seed and that he could not see it.

He pointed to a fig tree and added that the finest essence, which he could not even see, was the life of that fig tree.

He told him that the finest essence made up the self of the whole world: the truth, the self, him.

Svetaketu implored him to teach him more.

_____

_____

_____

_____

_____

_____

_____

_____

NOW TRY THIS!

- **Rewrite the dialogue as a play script.**

Teachers' note Remind the children of their previous work on the different ways of writing dialogue. You could introduce the terms direct speech and reported or indirect speech (see notes on the activities on page 11). Ask them which words they will change and how they know which ones to put within the speech marks.

A Lesson for Every Day
Literacy
9–10 Years
© A&C Black

Put yourself in their place: 1

Read this extract from a report. It is about children working in the potteries in the 19th century.

Each man employs two boys, one to turn the jigger, or wheel, from morning to night; the other to carry the ware just formed from the 'whirler' to the hot-house and moulds back. These hot-houses are rooms within rooms, closely confined except at the doors, and without windows. In the centre stands a large cast-iron stove, heated to redness, increasing the temperature often to 130 degrees. I have burst two thermometers at that point. During this inclement season I have seen these boys running to and fro on errands, or to their dinners, without stockings, shoes or jackets, and with perspriation standing on their foreheads, after labouring like slaves, with the mercury 20 degrees below freezing. The results of such transitions are soon realised, and many die of consumption, asthma, and acute inflammations.

From Mr Samuel Scriven's Report on the Staffordshire Potteries, 1843

Work in a group. Talk about what it would have been like to work in the potteries. Make notes on the cards.

How would you feel on your way to work?	. . . when you were at work?
. . . when you get home	How would you behave towards your master?

NOW TRY THIS!

- **Imagine you are a boy working in the factory and you start to feel ill.**
- **With a partner, role-play a conversation between the boy and his employer.**

chers' note Give each child a copy of this page. If this aspect of Victorian history has not been died, take time to discuss what the life of working children must have been like, and how their ployers might have treated them (see notes on the activity on page 11). Stress that this is a true ort, and explain that the author, Mr Samuel Scriven, wanted to help change the law. See also 'Put urself in their place: 2' on page 70.

A Lesson for Every Day
Literacy
9-10 Years
© A&C Black

Put yourself in their place: 2

- **Read these people's views.**

John

> I'm eight and I work 14 hours a day, Children like me don't go to school – that's just for rich families.

John's mother

> My youngest son works in the potteries. I don't like it, but we need the money he brings in. We have barely enough food as it is

Pottery owner

> If my workers want to employ children, that's their business. I have a factory to run and I can't afford to be soft.

Mr. Scriven

> These children risk their lives every time they go to work. We need new laws to improve their working conditions

- **Work in a group of four. Each take one of the characters.**
- **Put yourself in the character's place. Make notes about their views and the reasons for them.**

Character _____

My views

Why I think this

- **In role, discuss whether there should be new laws about children working in the potteries.**

NOW TRY THIS!

- **What do you think about the problem? Write a report of how this activity has helped you to develop your views.**

Teachers' note The children should first complete the activity on 'Put yourself in their place: 1'. Give each child a copy of this page and explain that the people shown are from the 1840s. Encourage the children to put aside their own personal views and feelings in order to explore the issue from their character's point of view.

A Lesson for Every Day
Literacy
9-10 Years
© A&C Black

Asif's viewpoint: 1

The story is set during a war in Afghanistan.

During the fighting Parvana and her father were separated from her mother and sister. Then her father died. Now Parvana is travelling across the country to find her mother and sister. She is carrying a baby boy she found in a burnt-out house.

Parvana has just come across a cave, which she thinks would be a good place to shelter.

"Get out of my cave!"

Parvana spun around and was running away before the voice stopped echoing off the cave walls. Fear kept her legs moving long after she was exhausted. When she finally slowed down, her brain began to tell her something she had been too scared to hear moments earlier. The voice that had yelled at her from the back of the cave was a child's voice.

Parvana stopped running and caught her breath. She turned around and looked back at the cave. She wasn't going to let some child keep her from getting a few days of rest!

"Let's go and see who's in there," she said to Hassan.

She went back to the mouth of the cave.

"Hello," she called in.

"I told you to get out of my cave!" the voice shouted. It was definitely a child's voice.

"How do I know it's your cave?" Parvana asked.

"I've got a gun. Go away or I'll shoot you."

Parvana hesitated. Lots of young boys in Afghanistan did have guns. But if he had a gun, why hadn't he shot at her already? "I don't believe you," Parvana said. "I don't think you're a killer. I think you're a kid just like me."

She took a few more steps forward, trying to see in the dark. A stone hit her on the shoulder.

"Stop that!" she shouted. "I'm carrying a baby."

"I warned you to stay away."

"All right, you win," Parvana said. "Hassan and I will leave you alone. We just thought you'd like to share our meal, but I guess you'd rather throw stones."

There was a moment's silence.

"Leave the food and go."

"I have to cook it first," Parvana said over her shoulder as she walked away. "If you want it, come out and get it."

Parvana put down the baby where she could watch him and kept talking while she gathered dried grasses and stalks from dead weeds for a cook fire. The water in the stream was clear and moving swiftly, so she thought it would be safe to drink without boiling it first. She dipped in her pan. "Here's some lovely cool water to drink, Hassan," she said. "Tastes good, doesn't it? Drink it all down, and we'll have a hot tasty supper." She gave him a piece of stale naan to keep him quiet until the meal was ready.

Parvana heard a little shuffling noise. Out of the corner of her eye she saw a small boy peering out from the cave. He was sitting on the ground. She took him some water.

Teachers' note The children should read this page and then, using 'Asif's viewpoint: 2' to help, rewrite from Asif's point of view. Help them to notice the clues that it is written from Parvana's point of view: expresses her thoughts and what she notices and is based on what she knows and does not know (for example, she does not know who is in the cave and tries to find out).

A Lesson for Every Day
Literacy
9–10 Years
© A&C Black

• **Rewrite the passage from *Parvana's Journey* from Asif's point of view** The first paragraph has been done for you.

"Get out of my cave!"

Asif smiled to himself. He had scared the girl who had the cheek to come into his cave. She was running away before his voice stopped echoing off the cave walls. She slowed down, looking exhausted.

> Show Asif's thoughts and feelings, but not Parvana's.

> Think about what Asif knows but Parvana does not.

> Think about what Parvana knows but Asif does not.

Continue on the back of the sheet if you need to.

NOW TRY THIS!

• **Reread what you have written.**
• **Have you shown why the boy was so unfriendly towards Parvana?**
• Edit **and improve your story.**

Teachers' note Use this with 'Asif's viewpoint: 1'. Having identified the clues that the passage was written from Parvana's point of view, the children can then consider how to alter it so that it represents Asif's point of view: expressing his thoughts and what he notices and basing it on what he knows (for example, he does not know who is outside the cave).

A Lesson for Every Day
Literacy
9–10 Years
© A&C Black

War zone research

- Use this page to prepare for writing a $\boxed{\text{story}}$ set in a war zone.

Use the Internet.

Find out about life for children who live there.

- Write $\boxed{\text{notes}}$.

How war affects the neighbourhood

- shops
- roads
- transport

How war affects the family's home

- damage
- evacuation

How war affects the family

- work
- separation
- injury

How war affects friendships

- separation
- new friends

How war affects school

- danger
- closure
- teachers

How war affects daily life

- food
- clothes
- leisure

NOW TRY THIS!

- **Write three questions you would like to ask a child who lives in a war zone.**

Teachers' note The children should first have completed 'Asif's viewpoint: 1 and 2', which depict a war zone (Afghanistan). Different children or different groups could research each aspect of the war zone, using the Internet sources suggested in Notes on the activities (see page 11) or others. Point out that authors need to find out about setting and culture in order to write a convincing story.

A Lesson for Every Day
Literacy
9-10 Years
© A&C Black

Letter from a war zone

- **Write a** `letter` **from a child in a war zone to tell a pen-friend what has been happening there.**
- **Write in the** `first person` **.**

> Use your research about war zones to help.

Your address _____

_____

_____

Date _____

Dear _____

When I woke up this morning _____

_____

_____

> Say how war has affected the child's neighbourhood, family, friends, home, school and daily life.

_____

_____

_____

_____

_____

_____

_____

_____

_____

I hope _____

Best wishes from your friend

_____

NOW TRY THIS!

- **Write a reply to the letter.**
- **Ask some questions about it.**

Teachers' note Having researched a war zone, the children use the information they have found to support their writing – imagining they are a child living in a war zone who is writing about his or her experiences.

A Lesson for Every Day
Literacy
9–10 Years
© A&C Black

Agra mystery: 1

- **Plan a story about a character who goes to Agra, in India, for a holiday.**
- **Make** notes **about what you need to know.**

The Taj Mahal is in Agra

A map of India

The character makes friends with Nimesh and Meena, a brother and sister who live in Agra. The opening of one chapter has been planned for you.

Story plan	What I need to know
Opening	
Something happens Character playing in courtyard of Nimesh and Meena's house. Look up as 6 green parrots (rose-ringed parakeets) suddenly squawk and fly out of cypress tree. What had scared them? Boy hiding in tree.	What are houses like in Agra? What kinds of tree grow there? What do they look and smell like? What kinds of bird live in the city? What do they look like? Where might you see them?
A problem develops	
The problem is resolved	
Ending	

NOW TRY THIS!

- **Do the research for your story.**
- **Make notes.**

Useful websites:
http://en.wikipedia.org/wiki/Agra
www.agraindia.org.uk

Teachers' note Copy this onto A3 paper. Ask the children what they know about Agra. Tell them the history of the Taj Mahal. Point out the map and ask them to find Agra on a map in an atlas. They could make notes about anything they find out. Tell them they are going to plan a story set in Agra and they need to research this setting. Remind them how to make notes quickly.

Agra mystery: 2

- **Write a paragraph for your story set in Agra, India.**
- **Base it on the notes.**
- **Use your research to help with details.**

Notes

Character playing in courtyard of Nimesh and Meena's house. Look up as 6 green parrots (rose-ringed parakeets) suddenly squawk and fly out of cypress tree. What had scared them?
Boy hiding in tree.

Give the main character a name.

Say what the children are playing.

Write some dialogue as well as narrative.

Use interesting vocabulary to help readers to imagine the setting.

NOW TRY THIS!

- **Write the opening paragraph of the story, which comes before the one on this page.**
- **Say how the main character got to know Nimesh and Meena.**

Teachers' note The children should first have completed 'Agra mystery: 1'. Ask the children what they know about Agra. Tell them the history of the Taj Mahal. Point out the map and ask them to find Agra on a map in an atlas. They could make notes about anything they find out. Tell them they are going to plan a story set in Agra and they need to research this setting. Remind them how to make notes quickly.

76

A Lesson for Every Day
Literacy
9–10 Years
© A&C Black

Tell the story

- **Rewrite the** | dialogue | **as part of a story,
  without using** | speech marks |.

Example:

Lee asked Gemma what <u>she</u> <u>would</u> do. Gemma said that <u>she</u> <u>didn't</u> know and that <u>she</u> might tell Lara.

1 Who was at the door?

I don't know.

Gemma   Lee

2 I can't see anyone.

I'll put the chain on and open the door.

3 I'll come with you.

I'm not scared.

4 We need to be careful.

I suppose you're right.

1 _____

_____

2 _____

_____

_____

3 _____

_____

4 _____

_____

NOW TRY THIS!

- **Write this dialogue as sentences.**

Will you open the door by yourself?

No.

Gemma   Lee

Teachers' note The children should first have completed page 76. Remind them that some research notes had been filled in for them on page 76 and are repeated here, and model how to fill out the notes into a story passage.

A Lesson for Every Day
Literacy
9-10 Years
© A&C Black

77

Dialogue to recount

- **Write the** dialogue **as sentences without** speech marks **.**

Notice what else you need to change.

"We'll be there in ten minutes," said Sam, as he looked at his watch.

"I can see the cathedral tower. It must be very old," said Pia.

"Yes – more than a thousand years," added Dad.

"When was it built?" asked Pia.

"I think it was built in 1093 and it took 40 years to complete," said Dad.

Sam said, "I didn't know they could build things like that such a long time ago."

"It was built for the shrine of St Cuthbert," said Dad as he rummaged about in his bag.

"How do you know so much about it?" asked Pia.

"I paid attention to what I was taught at school," he answered.

Sam smiled and said to Dad, "Maybe the guide book in your bag is a bit of help too."

_____

_____

_____

_____

_____

_____

_____

_____

_____

NOW TRY THIS!

- **Highlight the parts of the dialogue you changed.**
- **Explain to a partner why you changed these.**

78

Teachers' note Remind the children of the two ways of writing down what people say. Model how to change the first sentence to reported speech. Draw out the need to change the verb in the quotation to the past tense, add the word *that* and move the speaker's name to the beginning of the sentence. Note that *said to X that* can be changed to *told X*.

A Lesson for Every Day
Literacy
9–10 Years
© A&C Black

Two-way sentences

• Use | punctuation | marks to give each sentence two different meanings.

.	,	!	?	" "
full stop	comma	excamation mark	question mark	speech marks

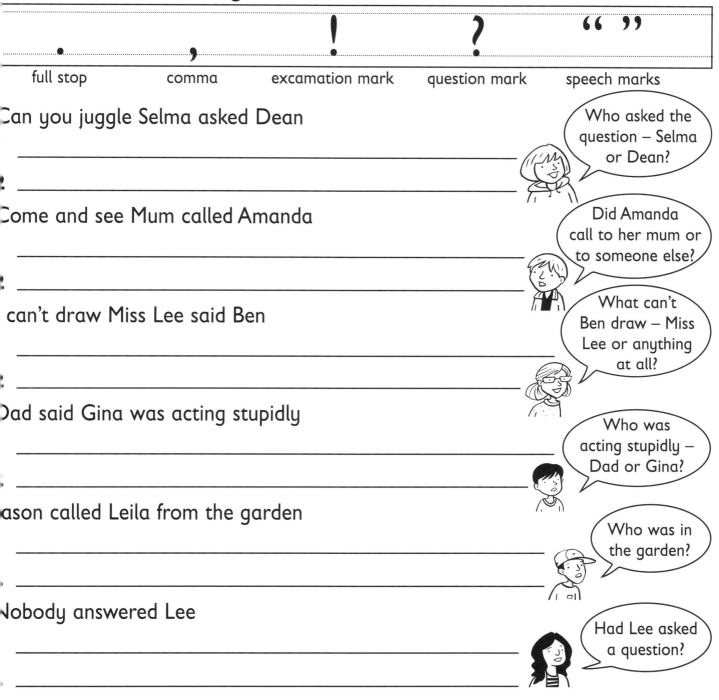

Can you juggle Selma asked Dean

_____

_____

Who asked the question – Selma or Dean?

Come and see Mum called Amanda

_____

_____

Did Amanda call to her mum or to someone else?

can't draw Miss Lee said Ben

_____

_____

What can't Ben draw – Miss Lee or anything at all?

Dad said Gina was acting stupidly

_____

_____

Who was acting stupidly – Dad or Gina?

ason called Leila from the garden

_____

_____

Who was in the garden?

Nobody answered Lee

_____

_____

Had Lee asked a question?

NOW TRY THIS!

• **Read your sentences aloud with a partner.**
• **Explain what each one means.**

eachers' note Tell the children that in this activity they are going to think of two ways in which to unctuate a sentence to give it two different meanings. They could try out their ideas on a notepad nd ask a partner to read them aloud.

LIVERPOOL JOHN MOORES UNIVERSITY
LEARNING SERVICES

A Lesson for Every Day
Literacy
9-10 Years
© A&C Black

Brackets wrap-up

- **Wrap the extra information in** | brackets |.
- **Squeeze it into the sentence.**

brackets

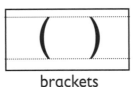
Add that Liverpool were playing Arsenal.

We went to the football match on Saturday.

We went to the football match (Liverpool versus Arsenal) on Saturday.

1 Please pass me the book from the table.

_____

_____

Add that you want the blue book.

2 Ask Heba to show you how to do it.

_____

_____

Add that Heba is a girl and is wearing a blue dress.

3 Henry VIII married six times.

_____

_____

Add that Henry ruled from 1509 to 1547.

4 Key in your PIN after inserting your card.

_____

_____

Add that PIN means Personal Identification Number.

NOW TRY THIS!

- **Add information in brackets to these sentences:**

    Mrs Ray asked the children to open their books.

    After his holiday Iain went to stay with his grandparents.

Teachers' note For this activity you need to record extracts from five radio programmes for different audiences, as listed. The children might identify some of them as suitable for more than one group of people. Ask them to say why. They could then compile lists of language and other features that make a radio programme suitable for each group of people.

A Lesson for Every Day
Literacy
9–10 Years
© A&C Black

Tune in

Listen to five radio broadcasts.
Decide who the programmes are for:

Work with a group.

| children under 4 | children of about your age | teenagers or young adults | older people | families 1·45 |

Write your group's answers on the chart.

Think about tone of voice, vocabulary, style of language.

Programme	Who it is for	How we can tell
1		
2		
3		
4		
5		

NOW TRY THIS!

- Share your answers with another group.
- Make a list of points you would need to think about if you made a radio programme for younger children.

eachers' note For this activity you need to record extracts from five radio programmes for different diences, as listed. The children might identify some of them as suitable for more than one group of ople. Ask them to say why. They could then compile lists of language and other features that make adio programme suitable for each group of people.

A Lesson for Every Day
Literacy
9-10 Years
© A&C Black

81

In trouble!

- **Imagine you have been in trouble at school. Make up the situation.**

How I got in trouble at school
When
Where
What happened and why

Idea bank

I kicked a ball and smashed a window.

I did not hand in my homework.

I snapped a ruler in half.

I climbed a tree and tore my short

You are going to explain what happened and why.

- **Choose one of these people to explain to. Think about whether you will use formal or informal language.**

 Parent or guardian

Friend

Headteacher

- **Now work in a group.**
- **Give your explanation. Ask the group to decide who they think you are explaining to.**
- **Ask your group how they could tell.**

NOW TRY THIS!

- **Work with a partner. Role-play a conversation with your headteacher where you use** informal **language.**

How will the headteacher react?

Teachers' note Discuss that different situations call for different kinds of language – formal or informal. The children should work in groups of four to six. You could write the three choics (parent or guardian/friend/headteacher) on slips of paper and put them in a bag; ask each child to draw from the bag to determine who they will be explaining to.

A Lesson for Every Day
Literacy
9–10 Years
© A&C Black

An older novel

Title _____

Author _____ Year _____

End of chapter summaries

Chapter	Main events	My questions	My predictions
1			
2			
3			
4			
5			

NOW TRY THIS!

- **Describe any surprises you had while reading the novel.**

Oh!

Teachers' note Use this page to help the children to write a reading journal of an older novel that is read in serial form. At the end of each chapter arrange a plenary session during which the children summarise what has happened so far, any queries they have and what they think might happen next.

A Lesson for Every Day
Literacy
9–10 Years
© A&C Black

Just William

- **Rewrite the passage so that it could belong in a *Just William* story.**
- **Make it sound more** old-fashioned .

Think about old and modern language.

Think about new inventions.

Waiting for Christmas

"What are you getting for Christmas?" asked William.

"Some sound things from my dad," said Ginger, "like an MP3 player and a new mobile. They're wicked. But my auntie's knitted me a sad green jumper and I know my mum's going to make me wear it. I should be grateful but I'll look such a loser."

William and Ginger usually spent the week before Christmas poking around in cupboards and drawers. They always found the presents their families had hidden.

"I found a load of stuff in the cupboard under the stairs," said William. "I'm getting a new mobile, too, and there's a wicked pair of trainers."

"Nothing to make you cringe?" asked Ginger.

"Yeah – a woolly hat with a bobble. Why do aunties knit things?" replied William.

"I dunno," said Ginger, "They could just cut out the middle man and give us the money. But I can't complain. I've only got £6.50, so I can't buy them anything cool."

"We could make pressies," suggested William, "like sweets. My mum's got loads of cookery books and all the stuff's in the kitchen. We could do it while she's in town tomorrow."

"Sound," said Ginger. "See you then."

NOW TRY THIS!

- **Write the next paragraph in the same old-fashioned style.**

Teachers' note The children need to have read some *Just William* stories so that they are familiar with the setting and the author's style. This passage is based on a *Just William* story but is written as if in the present day. Discuss how they can tell. Ask them about the differences between modern language and the language used in *Just William*. Draw out differences in vocabulary and formality.

A Lesson for Every Day
Literacy
9–10 Years
© A&C Black

Colon leaders

Link each beginning to an ending.
Write the sentences.
Put a | colon | in each one.

colon

Beginnings	Endings
We heard a scratching sound in the corner	how to swim.
They had three tasks	it had to be mice or rats. 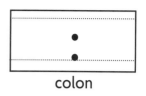
There was something she had to find out	the knave of hearts.
Alex saw a strange sight	Lucy, Meera and Aisha.
They knew who had stolen the tarts	to find the golden key, open the box and remove the jewels.
Their father taught them an important skill	who had been living in the old hut.
He had three sisters	Mr Carr dressed as a highwayman.

NOW TRY THIS!

• **Write endings for these sentences:**
He had three wishes
What we saw terrified us

Use colons.

chers' note Remind the children of their previous learning about colons and point out that a
on can be placed after a clause which introduces something else. Draw out that the first part of the
tence makes readers want to ask a question and that the second clause answers it.

A Lesson for Every Day
Literacy
9–10 Years
© A&C Black

Semi-colon connections

- **Put** ⟨ semi-colons ⟩ **in the sentences to make better sense.**

⟨ ; ⟩

semi-colon

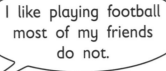

I like playing football most of my friends do not.

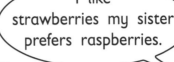

The woods were full of pheasants however on the moors we only saw grouse.

It will soon be Christmas after that I can have a rest.

I like strawberries my sister prefers raspberries.

On the fifth day of Christmas my true love sent to me five gold rings four calling birds three french hens and a partridge in a pear tree.

A first-class ticket will cost £300 a standard ticket will cost £12.

She had a Liverpool accent she supported Everton football club she was a Beatles fan yet she said she was a Londoner.

I'd like two fish and chips with peas a tuna salad with mayonnaise and a pizza with beans, please.

No-one lives in the house no-one seems to visit it but there is always rubbish in the bin.

NOW TRY THIS!

- **Continue these sentences. Use semi-colons:**

On the way to school

The Smiths are going to Italy in July

Teachers' note Read the first example aloud as it is written, with no punctuation except at the end. Ask the children if it sounds right. Discuss how the meaning could be made clearer using a semi-colon. Draw out that the two clauses could be written as separate sentences but that their meanings are linked. A semi-colon does not separate them as much as a full stop would.

A Lesson for Every Day
Literacy
9–10 Years
© A&C Black

Apostrophe alert

Put in the missing apostrophes .

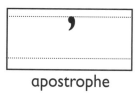

,

apostrophe

Toms Midnight Garden

Philippa Pearce

Jo Giants Missing Boot

Toni Goffe

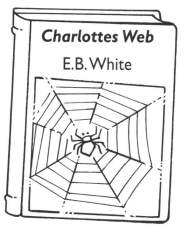

Charlottes Web

E.B. White

Alices Adventures in Wonderland

Lewis Carroll

Mother Gooses Tales

Old Possums Book of Practical Cats

T. S. Eliot

The Fairies Adventures

Titania Flowerbell

The Lighthouse Keepers Lunch

Ronda and David Armitage

Gullivers Travels

Jonathan Swift

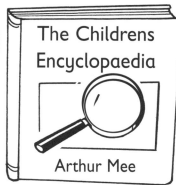

The Childrens Encyclopaedia

Arthur Mee

The Witchs Daughter

Nina Bawden

Loves Labours Lost

William Shakespeare

The Three Bears Home

Goldilocks

NOW TRY THIS!

- **Choose three book titles which have apostrophes for different reasons.**
- **Explain why each one has an apostrophe.**
- **Write your answers.**

achers' note Remind the children of their previous learning about apostrophes. Ask them where
ey are useful. Tell them that in this activity they are going to use apostrophes to show belonging or
nership in book titles.

A Lesson for Every Day
Literacy
9–10 Years
© A&C Black

Punctuation program

The computer has a bug.
It takes out all the | punctuation marks | .

- **Read the story below.**
- **Put in the punctuation marks.**

. , ? ! " " ' : ; — - ( )

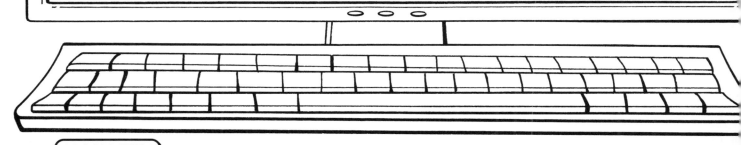

There was once a woman who had a son named Suan Each morning Suan climbed the tree near his home As soon as his mother came from the market Suan rushed home When she came in he cried Mother I know what you bought in the market He then told her article by article His mother began to believe he had skills as a diviner

One day the *datus daughters ring disappeared Everyone searched for it but in vain The datu said that any man who could find it could marry her Suans mother took Suan to the datu

Well Suan tomorrow tell me where the ring is said the datu

Suan asked the datu to give him his soldiers for the night the datu agreed Suan told the soldiers to stand in a semicircle He pointed at each of them saying The ring is here, and nowhere else One soldier trembled and became pale

I know who has it said Suan Then he told them to go to bed

During the night a soldier the one who had turned pale came to Suan and said I will get the ring you are in search of and will give it to you if you will promise me my safety

Give it to me, and you shall be safe said Suan

*datu: the chief of a tribe   Adapted from *Filipino Popular Tales* by Dean S. Fansler

NOW TRY THIS!

- **Choose three different punctuation marks.**
- **Explain why you used them.**

Tell a partner.

Teachers' note Ask the children to read the passage and to begin by marking the ends of sentences with full stops, exclamation marks or question marks. Once they have separated the sentences they can read each one carefully and decide if it needs any other punctuation.

A Lesson for Every Day
Literacy
9–10 Years
© A&C Black

All cued up

- **Cut out the cue cards.**
- **Write notes on them to help you to tell a story or present a talk.**

Think about...

...key words and phrases...

...making the content funny or interesting...

...when to pause...

...when to recap...

Teachers' note Model how to complete a cue card to help to tell a story or present a factual talk. The children should make notes on how to tell the story or present the talk: when to use recap (for example, the audience might need to be reminded of key points), where to inject humour (for example, to keep the audience's attention) and which words, phrases or sentences to repeat.

A Lesson for Every Day
Literacy
9–10 Years
© A&C Black

In the deep dark wood . . .

- **Read this story opening.**
  It is based on *Little Red Riding Hood*.

> In the very darkest corner of the deep dark wood sat the Big Bad Girl.
>
> The Big Bad Girl was just about as BIG and BAD as a girl can be, and all the woodland animals were afraid of her. She hung about beside the forest path and carved her name on trees. She shouted rude things at any little animal who passed by. The Big Bad Girl tripped up little deer. She stole fir cones from baby squirrels and threw them at the poor hedgehogs. The woodland birds didn't dare to sing when the Big Bad Girl was around! But the person the Big Bad Girl liked to tease most of all was a charming little wolf cub who often passed by on his way to visit dear Old Granny Wolf.
>
> Little Wolfie was the sweetest, fluffiest, politest little cub you could ever hope to meet. He would run along the path, skippty-skip, carrying a basket of freshly baked goodies for Old Granny Wolf, singing all the time.
>
> From *Little Red Riding Wolf* by Lawrence Anholt

The pictures show what happens in the rest of the story.

- **Make cue cards to help you tell the story.**
  Remember to use repetition and
  humour, like in the story opening.

You need the sheet called *Give us a cue.*

- **Tell the story to your class or to your group**

Teachers' note Use this with 'All cued up'; give each child one copy of each page. First read the passage to the class and talk about how it is different from the traditioinal tale of *Little Red Riding Hood*. If any children are unfamiliar with the original story, recap the main events. Then look at the pictures together, pointing out that the children can make up extra plot detils.

A Lesson for Every Day
Literacy
9-10 Years
© A&C Black

Gory story

- **Read the beginning of this poem by Roald Dahl. It is based on *Cinderella*.**

Cinderella

I guess you think you know this story.
You don't. The real real one's much more gory.
The phoney one, the one you know,
Was cooked up years and years ago,
And made to sound all soft and sappy
Just to keep the children happy.
Mind you, they got the first bit right,
The bit where, in the dead of night,
The Ugly Sisters, jewels and all,
Departed for the Palace Ball,
While darling little Cinderella
Was locked up in a slimey cellar,
Where rat who wanted things to eat,
Began to nibble at her feet.

Roald Dahl.

- **Make notes about what you think will happen in the rest of the poem.**

What will happen next?	What will happen at the ball?
What will the prince do?	How will the poem end?

- **Retell the poem as a story. Make cue cards to help you tell it to the rest of the class.**

You need the sheet called *Give us a cue*.

Teachers' note Use this with 'All cued up'; give each child one copy of each page. Read the poem with the children and discuss what could happen next. Allow any suggestions, encouraging the children to adapt the traditional story in any way they wish. Point out that they are going to retell the poem as a story, so it does not need to rhyme.

A Lesson for Every Day
Literacy
9-10 Years
© A&C Black

'The Piano': scenes

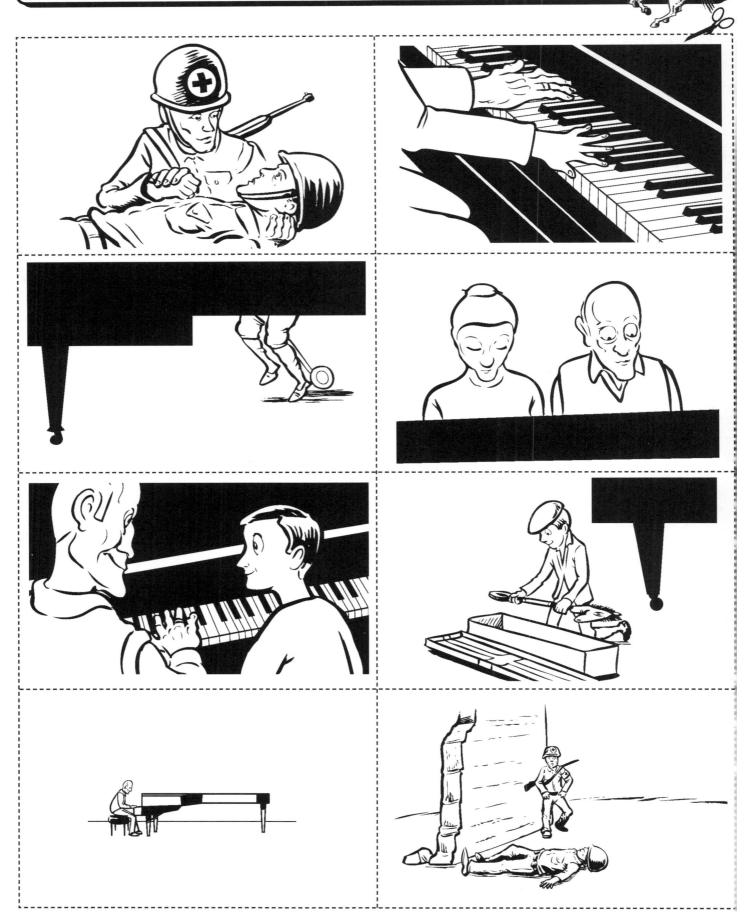

Teachers' note The children should first have watched, listened to and responded to the animated film The Piano by Aidan Gibbons (see notes on p.13). The children could use the pictures to help them tell the story, or they could put them in order of appearance in the film and then in chronological order to draw out that the story is told through flashbacks.

A Lesson for Every Day
Literacy
9-10 Years
© A&C Black

'The Piano': mood cards

anguished	calm	carefree
distressing	dreamlike	gentle
grim	happy	light-hearted
loving	melancholy	mournful
moving	mysterious	peaceful
quiet	romantic	sad
sorrowful	tender	touching
tranquil	warm	wistful
exciting	thrilling	horrific

Teachers' note The children should first have carried out the activity on page 92. Working in groups the children could cut out the cards and split them into sets: those that described the mood of the film and those that do not. They can then take the first set and begin to arrange them on a zone of relevance grid. Ask them to give evidence for each word they choose.

A Lesson for Every Day
Literacy
9-10 Years
© A&C Black

93

'The Piano': a life in a tune

• **Write the piano player's answers.**

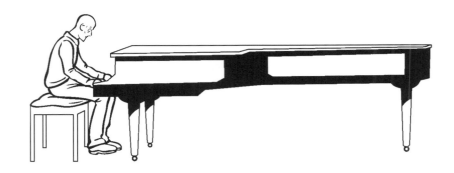

1 What is your very earliest memory?

_____

_____

_____

2 Who were your family?

_____

_____

3 What are your happiest memories?

_____

_____

4 What are your saddest memories?

_____

_____

NOW TRY THIS!

• **Make a time-line.**
• **Write some events from the piano player's life on it.**

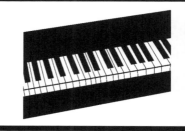

Teachers' note The children should first have carried out the activity on 'The Piano: scenes' and 'The Piano: mood cards'. Replay the film and think about the questions it answers (and any it leaves unanswered) about the man's life. After writing the questions the children could replay it to look for answers, supporting them with evidence from the film.

A **Lesson for Every Day**
Literacy
9–10 Years
© A&C Black

'The Piano': thoughts and words

• **Write what the characters are thinking and saying.**

• **Write a longer dialogue for one of the scenes.**

Teachers' note The children should first have carried out the activity on the other *The Piano* sheets. Replay the film to look more closely at the scenes shown here. The children could enact them with a partner (or alone, if easier), speaking the words or just thinking them. Remind them of the mood of the film (see 'The Piano: mood cards') and consider any words which better communicate this mood.

A Lesson for Every Day
Literacy
9–10 Years
© A&C Black

Evaluator

- **Colour the stars to show how well each** effect **in your 'life story' film worked.**

- **Explain your** evaluation .

Scene number and description	Effects	Evaluation: Not → Very effective	Explanation
1	Colour	☆ ☆ ☆ ☆ ☆	
	Facial expressions	☆ ☆ ☆ ☆ ☆	
	Movement	☆ ☆ ☆ ☆ ☆	
	Sound	☆ ☆ ☆ ☆ ☆	
2	Colour	☆ ☆ ☆ ☆ ☆	
	Facial expressions	☆ ☆ ☆ ☆ ☆	
	Movement	☆ ☆ ☆ ☆ ☆	
	Sound	☆ ☆ ☆ ☆ ☆	
3	Colour	☆ ☆ ☆ ☆ ☆	
	Facial expressions	☆ ☆ ☆ ☆ ☆	
	Movement	☆ ☆ ☆ ☆ ☆	
	Sound	☆ ☆ ☆ ☆ ☆	
4	Colour	☆ ☆ ☆ ☆ ☆	
	Facial expressions	☆ ☆ ☆ ☆ ☆	
	Movement	☆ ☆ ☆ ☆ ☆	
	Sound	☆ ☆ ☆ ☆ ☆	

NOW TRY THIS!

- **Which is the best** scene **of your film?**
- **How could you improve one other scene?**

Teachers' note Use this page after the children have made a short film of someone's life story. If their film has more than four scenes, provide a second copy of the page with the scene numbers masked. You may wish to enlarge the copies to A3 size to allow more room for the children's explanations of their evaluation scores.

A Lesson for Every Day
Literacy
9–10 Years
© A&C Black

Is this your life?

Write questions to [interview] **an older person you know about his or her life story. Write the answers.**

> Find out about important events in the person's life. Find out about happy and sad memories.

Person's name _____

What you already know about him or her _____

_____

Questions

Answers

Glue a picture of the person here

NOW TRY THIS!

• **Talk to a friend about how you could show this person's life in a** [film] **like *The Piano*.**

Teachers' note This could be used for homework. The children will plan a 'life story' film. The subject will be an older person they know. In class they could make notes on what they already know about the person and what they want to find out.

A Lesson for Every Day
Literacy
9–10 Years
© A&C Black

97

Life story

- **Plan a** [film] **about the life of an older person you know.**
- **Include five key events in the person's life.**
- **Make** [notes] **about what to show on the screen.**

Use *The Piano* as a model. The film can have music but no dialogue.

Key event	What you will show on the screen
1	
2	
3	
4	
5	

NOW TRY THIS!

- **Collect copies of photographs and other useful pictures to help: for example, important greetings cards, invitations and certificates.**

Teachers' note The children should first have completed 'Is this your life'. Ask them to read their notes and the interview notes and to pick out the five most important events in the person's life. How will they show these on screen as if in a film modelled on *The Piano*?

A Lesson for Every Day
Literacy
9–10 Years
© A&C Black

Biopic

- **Describe the five main** scenes **in your 'life story' film.**
- **Show how you will** link **the scenes.**

Film title _____
Subject _____
_____

Music _____
Why I chose it _____

Links can be people coming and going, the subject's thoughts, important objects and so on.

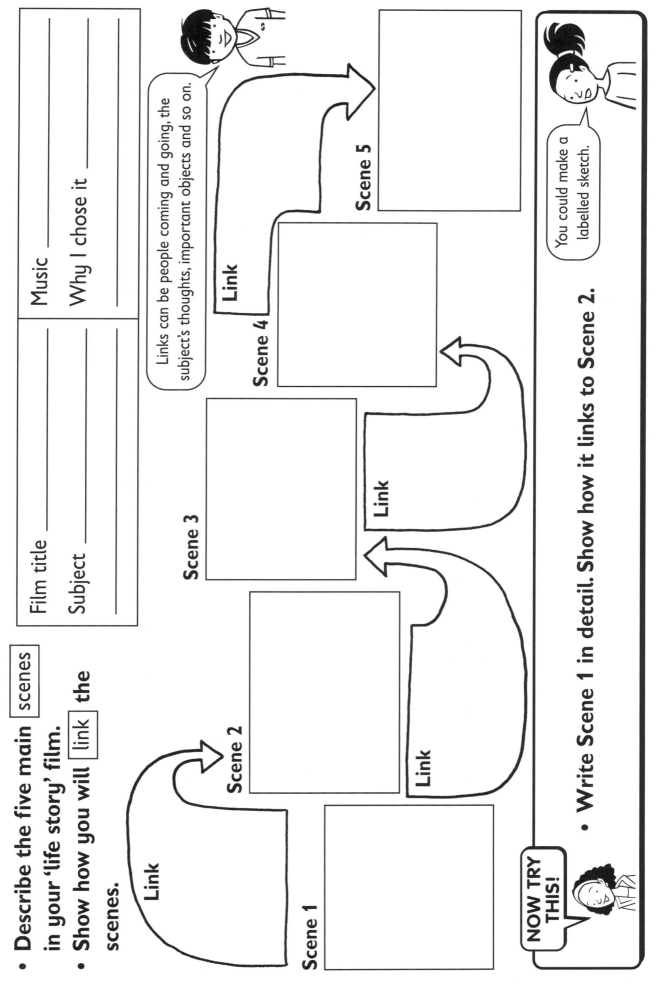

Scene 1

Link

Scene 2

Link

Scene 3

Link

Scene 4

Link

Scene 5

- **Write Scene 1 in detail. Show how it links to Scene 2.**

NOW TRY THIS!

You could make a labelled sketch.

teachers' note The children should first have completed 'Is this your life?'. They could first make notes about the images used in *The Piano* to depict key moments in the man's life and how these were linked (music, background changes, colour, costume changes). They should write notes in the boxes about the images they will show and write in the arrows how these will be linked.

Flagged up

- Write a statement using the words on the flags.
- Use the spare words as many times as you like.
- Do not add any other words.
- Write a question using the same words.
  The first one has been done for you.

Spare words

a   the   in   are

is   to   and

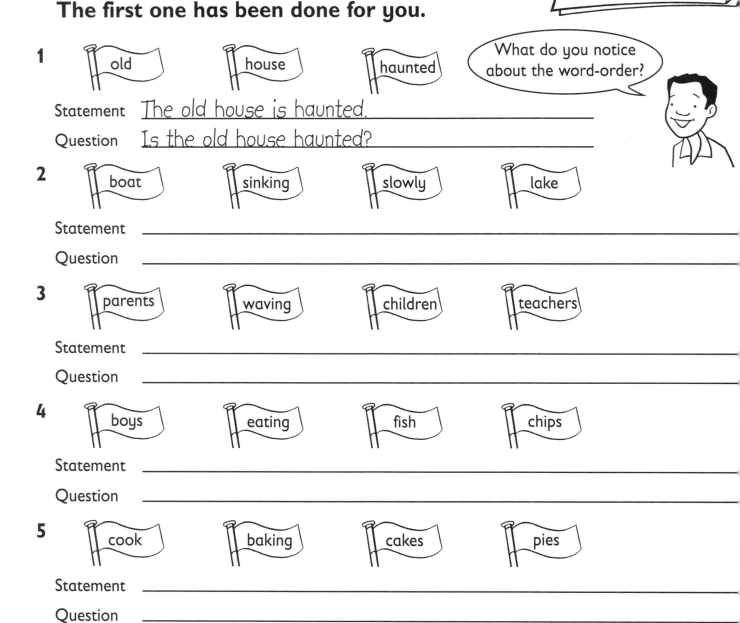

1   old   house   haunted   What do you notice about the word-order?

Statement   The old house is haunted.

Question   Is the old house haunted?

2   boat   sinking   slowly   lake

Statement _____

Question _____

3   parents   waving   children   teachers

Statement _____

Question _____

4   boys   eating   fish   chips

Statement _____

Question _____

5   cook   baking   cakes   pies

Statement _____

Question _____

NOW TRY THIS!

- Change the order of the words in each sentence to write a command .

You will need to change the form of the verbs.

Teachers' note Write up a statement: for example, *They are enjoying the film*. Ask the children what kind of sentence it is and invite them to change it into a question (*Are they enjoying the film?*). Ask them what changes they made: the full stop was exchanged for a question mark, the verb position was changed and the subject, they, was also moved.

A Lesson for Every Day
Literacy
9–10 Years
© A&C Black

Make it agree!

Underline the verbs that do not match the [nouns] or [pronouns].
Circle the verbs used in the wrong [tense].
Rewrite the sentences.

 They were all sat there watching me.

 I never done it.

It were raining when I came out.

_____
_____
_____

_____
_____
_____

_____
_____
_____

 She don't like going to the vet.

Dad said he seen that film ages ago.

 We was on holiday when it happened.

_____
_____
_____

_____
_____
_____

_____
_____
_____

I says to him, 'You can't sit there.'

You shouldn't have went in there.

Jen and Tom's going to Florida this year.

_____
_____
_____

_____
_____
_____

_____
_____
_____

 **NOW TRY THIS!**

- **Correct these and explain what makes them non-standard English:**

  Me and Jack's won.   The card was for Mum and I.

xchers' note It is useful to provide a sound or video recording of a radio or television programme which non-standard English is used frequently. Ask the children to listen for any expressions which e used in everyday conversation but which would not be correct in formal writing. The children _ld then give examples and then change them to standard English.

Sentence turn-around

- **Change the order of the words in the sentences to give a different meaning.**

They saw an advertisement for the jumble sale in the post office.	→	They saw an advertisement. It was for the jumble sale in the post office.
They saw an advertisement in the post office for the jumble sale.	→	They saw an advertisement in the post office. It was for the jumble sale

1 They performed a play written by Shakespeare in June.

_____

2 Swinging from branch to branch she saw the chimpanzees.

_____

3 I bought a book about whales in Luton.

_____

4 I heard all about the party last night.

_____

5 Emily told me that she had learned to swim on the way home from school.

_____

_____

NOW TRY THIS!

- **Explain the differences in meaning between each pair of sentences.**

Teachers' note Explain that sentences can make sense when the words are written in different orders but that this can change the meaning. Read the completed example and discuss what the first version could mean and how the second version is made clearer.

A Lesson for Every Day
Literacy
9–10 Years
© A&C Black

Clause squeeze

- **Squeeze the extra information into the sentences.**

Add a clause. It must contain a verb.

Surround the clause with commas.

Add a word to connect the clause.

James won the 100 metres.

James had his bag stolen.

James, who won the 100 metres, had his bag stolen.

The village had been flooded in the winter.

The village was full of cars

_____

_____

The dog had been reported missing.

She spotted the dog in the woods.

_____

_____

The volcano was thought to be extinct.

A volcano erupted in Italy.

_____

_____

The girl had tears in her eyes.

The girl struggled up the hill.

_____

_____

Dan was very tall.

Dan could reach the shelf.

_____

_____

NOW TRY THIS!

- **Add different clauses to three of the sentences.**

Teachers' note Explain that information can be added to a fiction or non-fiction text by adding extra sentences but that in some cases a clause giving extra information can be added to a sentence, making it longer. Model this using the completed example and point out that the commas help to communicate the meaning the writer intends.

A Lesson for Every Day
Literacy
9-10 Years
© A&C Black

103

Bedroom computer: 1

- **Cut out the statements about computers.**
- **Sort them into two sets: for and against having a computer in a child's bedroom.**

Parents need to keep an eye on which websites children are visiting.	If children are always supervised they never learn to be responsible for themselves.	It's difficult to do homework in the living room when others are chatting, watching television or listening to music.
A computer is useful for helping with homework.	It is harmful to children's health to use a computer for too long.	A family is a community that should be together in their spare time, rather than doing things in separate rooms.
Other people might be using the computer; the child might not often get the chance to use it.	Younger children in the family might be playing in the living room when the older child needs peace and quiet to use the computer for homework.	Children can keep in touch with their friends through networking sites.
Parents need to know who their children are talking to in chat rooms.	Children need to be active; having a computer in the bedroom encourages them to sit still for hours.	Parents should trust their children.
Children resent parents watching everything they do.	If children are using the computer in a suitable way they should not worry about using it in a family room.	If adults have important work to do on the computer the child will not get a chance to use it.
Families can find ways of sharing a computer fairly.	It is difficult to share a computer if more than one person has something important to do.	Buying an extra computer is expensive. Sharing one leaves money for other things.

NOW TRY THIS!

- **Talk to a partner about how you would argue for having a computer in your bedroom.**

Teachers' note Working in a group or pair to sort the cards ensures that the children talk about the ideas. This can also be useful for those who need help in reading them. After sorting them they could each pick out one (or possibly more) they agree with and one (or more) they disagree with, and say why.

A Lesson for Every Day
Literacy
9–10 Years
© A&C Black

Bedroom computer: 2

- **Role-play an argument between a child who wants a computer in his or her bedroom and a parent who disagrees.**
- **Use some of the statements you have sorted into sets.**
- **Then write notes for your argument in the speech bubbles.**

eachers' note The children should first have completed 'Bedroom computer: 1'. They select tatements to support the argument of the child or the parent and complete the page in pairs: one working on the child's argument, the other on the parent's. They should work together, answering ach other.

A Lesson for Every Day
Literacy
9–10 Years
© A&C Black

Keeping active: 1

- Talk together about what you think you should do to keep active.
- Write your important words in the ovals.
- Draw lines to connect the ones that are linked.
- Write sentences to connect them.

Check that everyone has equal opportunities to say something.

How to keep active

Each day try to

go for a walk

or

go for a run

NOW TRY THIS!

- Talk together about what you already do and what else you could do.
- Write a list.

Teachers' note Use this to elicit the children's ideas about keeping active before beginning work on the topic (use it again at the end of the unit of work to involve them in assessing what they have learned). The group must agree on what is written. Ask them to choose a representative to visit other groups to hear their ideas and then report back.

A Lesson for Every Day
Literacy
9–10 Years
© A&C Black

Keeping active: 2

- **Decide on one thing you can all do to become more active.**
- **It must be realistic – check with your teacher!**

Work in a group of four.

Our keeping active plan	
We are going to	
How we shall do this	

Actions for each member of our group	
Name	Action

How we shall check how well we are doing:

_____

_____

NOW TRY THIS!

- **Make a checklist that you can use to check your progress.**
- **The group must agree on it.**

Teachers' note This page can be used to support the children with a plan of action for keeping active. They should first have researched their idea and agreed with you that it is feasible. They will also need to decide, with help, when to carry out a check of how well they are doing in keeping to their plan. See also 'Keeping active: 3'.

A Lesson for Every Day
Literacy
9–10 Years
© A&C Black

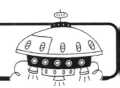

- **Use this page to plan a report to the class about your group's keeping active project.**
- **The group should agree on what to write.**

You should have used the plan called **Our keeping active plan**.

Report notes		
What we planned		
What we each did		
Name	Action	Result
What has worked well		What has not worked so well, and why

NOW TRY THIS!

- **With your group, plan and write a 'press statement' about your project.**
- **This should be just one sentence.**

Teachers' note Use this with 'Keeping active: 2'. It provides a format to help the children to record and review their progress in their 'keeping active' plan and to make changes where necessary. They should carry out their review as a group, with one acting as group leader and another as scribe.

A Lesson for Every Day
Literacy
9–10 Years
© A&C Black

Group roles

Work in a group.

- **Talk together about what each group role means in a discussion.**
- **Write the actions each member should take.**
- **Some actions will be taken by more than one member.**

Leader

Mentor

Scribe

Reporter

Actions bank

ask
challenge
collect ideas
decide
describe
encourage
explain
help
inform
instruct
listen
make notes
organise
persuade
plan
present
question
read aloud
share ideas
suggest
summarise
support
tell
time
write

NOW TRY THIS!

- **Write three examples of how each group member can carry out their role well.**

Teachers' note Give the children about two minutes to talk to a partner about what each group role entails. They can then share their ideas with the group and agree on a list of actions for each group role.

A Lesson for Every Day
Literacy
9–10 Years
© A&C Black

109

Cinderella panto: 1

- **Read the opening scene of the pantomime *Cinderella*.**
- **Work in a group. Discuss what the characters are like. How does the writer make the scene funny?**

Scene: the kitchen. Cinderella is dressed in rags, asleep. Her two pet mice are cuddled up with her. Buttons enters, steps to the front of the stage and looks out at the audience.

Buttons: Hello, everyone out there.

Audience: Hello.

Buttons *(putting his hand to his ear)*: I can't hear you. You can do better than that!

Audience *(shouting)*: Hello!

Buttons: That's better. Is everyone happy this afternoon? Well, we'll soon put a stop to that! So, here we are in the house of stupid Baron Hardup. He married the dreadful Sinistra and now Cinderella has been put to work in the kitchen as a slave. And I like her . . . *(bashfully)* . . . a lot! *(Shreiking is heard from the wings.)* Oh no, here comes the dreadful Sinnistra. *(The Dame enters.)*

Dame: What are you doing here, you snivelling little rat?

Audience: Oooooooo!

Dame *(moving to the front of the stage)*: And you can all shut up . . . *(growls)*

Audience: Booooooo!

Buttons: I'm doing my chores, madam.

Dame: What chores? *(sounds like 'What's yours?')*

Buttons: Oh thanks – mine's a cup of coffee and a chocolate biscuit! *(The Dame hits him around the head and chases him.)*

Cinderella *(waking up)*: Oh no, my wicked stepmother is bothering Buttons again. *(The two mice trip up the dame and she falls into a vat of custard.)*

- **Decide who will play each of the three characters. The rest of the group should play the part of the audience.**
- **Perform the scene.**

 **NOW TRY THIS!**

- Improvise the rest of the scene. Make it as funny as you can.

 Remember to use actions and gestures.

 110 **Teachers' note** The children should work in groups of up to six. Give each child or pair a copy of this page and read the playscript to the children. Discuss the features of pantomime (see also 'Cinderella panto: 2'). When improvising the rest of the scene, encourage the children to think about how the characters would behave and react to one another. See also page 112.

A Lesson for Every Day
Literacy
9–10 Years
© A&C Black

Read the character list from the pantomime *Cinderella*.

Cinderella: the Pantomime
Cast of characters

Baron Hardup	The confrused and rather stupid father of Cinderella; owner of Hardup House, where most of the action takes place
Cinderella	Baron Hardup's beautiful daughter
Sinistra (the Dame)	The wicked stepmother – newly married to Baron Hardup
Gertrude and Griselda	The ugly sisters; Sinistra's daughters
Buttons	A kind servant at Hardup House; Cinderella's only friend there
Fairy Godmother	Cinderella's kind fairy godmother
Prince Michael	The handsome Prince (principal boy)
Dandini	The Prince's faithful friend
Two mice	Cinderella's pets in the kitchen (to be magically changed into footmen)

Work in a group. Talk about what you think the characters will be like. Which characters will be funny?

Choose part of the story of *Cinderella*. Write a playscript for this scene of the pantomime.

Remember to use stage directions

Decide who will play each part. Act the scene.

NOW TRY THIS!

- **Discuss how the stage directions helped you to act the scene.**
- **What other stage directions would be useful? Add them to your playscript.**

eachers' note The children should first complete the activity on 'Cinderella panto: 1', so that they are miliar with playscripts and the features of pantomimes. Give each child or pair a copy of this page. rst discuss how the stage directions in a playscript help the actors to convey appropriate feelings nd emotions when performing the scene. One child in the group should act as scribe.

A Lesson for Every Day
Literacy
9-10 Years
© A&C Black

Pantomime features

- **Read the passage about pantomime.**

Pantomime is a Christmas or New Year entertainment in Britain. The main characters are a principal boy and a heroine, which are both played by young women. The 'Dame' is played by a man! The plot is usually based on a folk tale, such as Puss in Boots or Cinderella.

The ingredients of pantomime include slapstick comedy (such as custard pies being thrown in people's faces), popular songs and audience participation. Everyone boos the villains and there are arguments between characters and the audience. In the end, the villains get what they deserve and the good characters live happily ever after.

- **Watch a pantomime performance. Look for examples of the features on the chart.**
- **Work with a partner. Make notes on the chart.**

Name of the pantomime _____

Feature	Examples from performance
Good characters	
Villains	
Slapstick comedy	
Popular songs	
Audience participation	

NOW TRY THIS!

- **Think about how a pantomime makes you feel. How is it different from other plays? Talk with a partner and make notes.**

Teachers' note Before the lesson, obtain a video recording of a pantomime (see notes on the activity, page 15). First read the passage with the children and encourage children who have been to a pantomime to describe what it was like. Compare this with other plays the children have seen. Then talk through the features on the chart before playing the recording. Share the children's ideas during the plenary session.

A Lesson for Every Day
Literacy
9-10 Years
© A&C Black

Word history

Complete the questions about these words with | irregular spellings |.
Look up the words in an etymological dictionary.
Write the answers in the speech bubbles.

breakfast

Why isn't it spelt **brekfast**?

Because it is a meal that **breaks** the night-time fast.

cupboard

Why isn't it spelt **cubboard**?

Because _____ _____ _____.

beauty

Why isn't it spelt _____?

Because _____ _____ _____.

sign

_____?

Because _____ _____ _____.

bureau

_____?

Because _____ _____ _____.

naughty

_____?

Because _____ _____ _____.

achers' note Read the first example to the children before giving them a copy of the page and ask
hey can think why breakfast might be spelt in this way (What might it mean?). Ask them to discuss
e meanings of the other words with strange spellings and to write their ideas. They can then check
eir answers in an etymological dictionary.

A Lesson for Every Day
Literacy
9–10 Years
© A&C Black

113

Prefix change

- **Change each** ⬚prefix⬚ **to make a new word.**

detach	→ attach	instruct	→
repel	→	imply	→
dislike	→	affect	→
extract	→	compartment	→
export	→	tricycle	→
reject	→	impact	→
inspect	→	unload	→
compose	→	ascend	→

NOW TRY THIS!

- **Use different prefixes to make new words from these base words.**

  press   tend

Write as many words as you can from each.

Teachers' note Ask the children for examples of prefixes. They could write or type these and they could be displayed for reference. Use the completed example to demonstrate how to complete the activity and ask the children to suggest prefixes for the second one. Point out that some base words can have several different prefixes: for example, *compel/dispel/expel/impel/repel*.

A Lesson for Every Day
Literacy
9–10 Years
© A&C Black

Segment sense

In the wedges write words containing the ⬚ segment ⬚ in the centre circle.

Try not to use a word more than once.

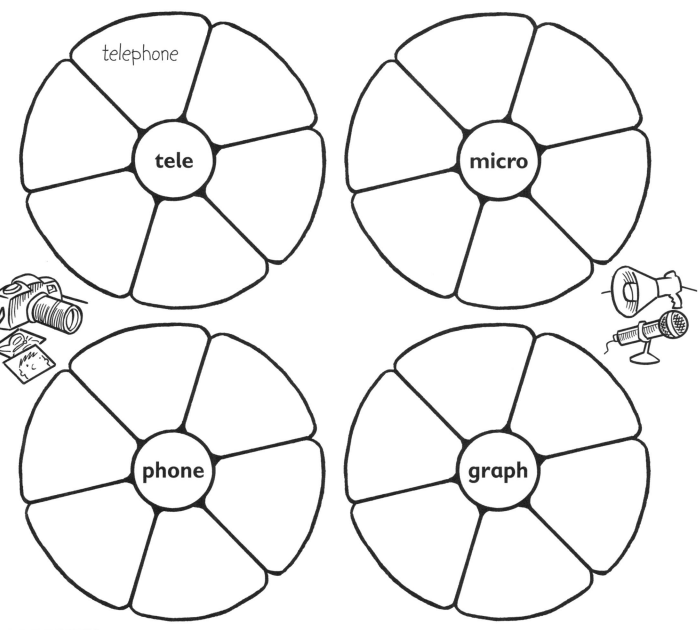

telephone

tele

micro

phone

graph

NOW TRY THIS!

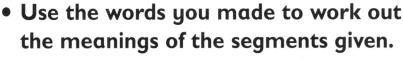

- **Use the words you made to work out the meanings of the segments given.**
- **Write definitions for four of the words (one for each segment).**

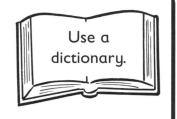

Use a dictionary.

achers' note Remind the children that words can be split in different ways to help with spelling:
o phonemes, syllables or segments that have a meaning. A segment might have one or more
llables. During the plenary, ask them to give the meanings of the words they made. Help them to
duce the meaning of each segment (see Notes on the activities, page 15).

A Lesson for Every Day
Literacy
9–10 Years
© A&C Black

Verbalise

- **Add the suffix** ise **to form verbs.**
- **List the verbs on the notepads.**
- **Give each list a heading to say whether the base word changed, and how.**

advice	criminal	liquid	pressure	sterile
central	immobile	magnet	private	terror
colony	legal	memory	serial	victim

Think about other suffixes and how they change base words. What similarities can you find?

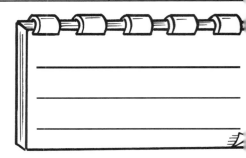

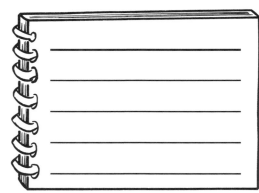

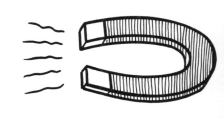

NOW TRY THIS!

- **Add the suffix** ise **to these words to form verbs.**

factor   item   plural   agony   category

harmony   fertile   energy   critic   stable

Teachers' note Begin with a clumsy sentence that has an incorrectly used noun or adjective that should be a verb and highlight the words to change: for example, *Mum said that we could not go on holiday this year because we must economy.* Ask the children to suggest a verb formed from economy (economise).

A Lesson for Every Day
Literacy
9-10 Years
© A&C Black

Script match

Match the │ scripts │ to the television programme types.
Explain your answers.

Think about person, tense, type of sentence and style of language.

1 After a cold start (between 1 and 2 degrees Celsius) the northeast of England will have a mainly sunny day.

2 A goal from Didier Drogba towards the end of extra time made the final score one nil – giving Chelsea victory over Manchester United in the first FA Cup final at the new Wembley stadium.

3 Have you ever wondered why some face creams are so expensive? Don't be fooled by fancy packaging…

4 Escomb is one of the most complete small Anglo-Saxon churches in England. It is not known exactly when the church was built but it is thought to be before AD700.

5 Fire-fighters rescued two children from a burning house in York after their mother called 999 at 5 am today.

6 Welcome to the show, Tony. Now, tell us about your invention. What does it do?

9 Under the dark water of the lake is a forest of green plants. Among them live countless fish…

7 Carragher heads the ball to Terry. Is he going to take a shot? Yes! What a save from Helton! So it's still England nil, Brazil nil, after 60 minutes.

8 Your two minutes start now – What is the largest artificial lake in Europe?

10 Now you can afford that new sofa – nothing to pay until August next year.

11 Traffic came to a standstill on the A1 north of Berwick today after a lorry shed its load.

Programme type	Script	How I can tell
News		
Advertisement		
Sports report		
Sports commentary		
Documentary		
Quiz show		
Chat show		
Weather forecast		

Teachers' note What do the children watch or listen to that has a script? Draw out that most non-fiction radio and television programmes, as well as plays, are based on scripts. Do they know any programmes which cannot be scripted beforehand? Look for clues to help match the scripts to the programmes: subject matter, person, tense, tone and connectives used.

A Lesson for Every Day
Literacy
9–10 Years
© A&C Black

117

In the script

- **Watch some** scripted **television extracts.**
- **Listen to some scripted radio extracts.**
- **Make notes about them on the chart.**

To entertain, inform, instruct or persuade.

Advertisement, chat show, documentary, news, quiz show, cooking or gardening programme, sports commentary or report, weather forecast.

Title	Type	Purpose

NOW TRY THIS!

- **Choose one extract.**
- **Explain how it is good for its purpose.**

Teachers' note Prepare for this activity by recording extracts from some different types of radio and television programmes (live or from the broadcasting companies' websites). After the children have identified the type of programme from the list provided, ask them to consider what each type of programme is for. Why do people watch or listen to it?

A Lesson for Every Day
Literacy
9–10 Years
© A&C Black

Leisure survey

What is there to do in your locality after school and at weekends?
Find out, so that you can plan
a [documentary] about it.
Make a note of each activity.

Ask others in the class what they know.

Ask other children.

Check in local newspapers.

Ask at leisure centres.

Check notices and leaflets in the library.

Check the local council's website.

Sports

Creative (art, craft, dance, drama)

Entertainment (cinema, theatre, etc.)

Social (clubs for various activities)

Outdoor activities (nature, history, geography)

Other (e.g. Scouts)

NOW TRY THIS!

- **What do you need to find out about each activity?**
- **Think about the information users will need.**

achers' note Introduce this activity with a short play (see notes on the activity on page 16). Tell the
ildren that they are going to prepare a short documentary about children's leisure facilities in their
ea. This can begin with a similar mini-play. Do they think there are many facilities? Ask them what
ey know about the different categories. They could share the task of finding out within their group.

A Lesson for Every Day
Literacy
9-10 Years
© **A&C Black**

Leisure documentary planner

- Collect information for a [documentary] about children's leisure activities in your locality.

Your group will research one type of activity.

- Contact the organisers by telephone, text or email.

- **Write** [notes].

Types of activity ✓

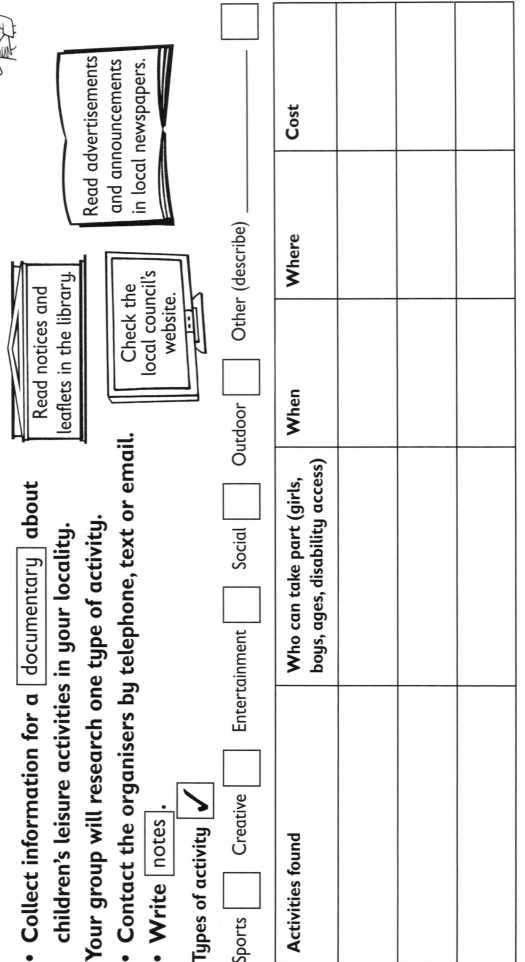

Read advertisements and announcements in local newspapers.

Read notices and leaflets in the library.

Check the local council's website.

	Sports	Creative	Entertainment	Social	Outdoor	Other (describe) _____

Activities found	Who can take part (girls, boys, ages, disability access)	When	Where	Cost

NOW TRY THIS!

- How can you present this information in a documentary on screen?
- Think about pictures, photographs, videos, illustrations, maps and diagrams.

Teachers' note Copy this onto A3 paper. The children should first have completed 'Leisure survey' and watched and discussed some television documentaries (see *100% New Developing Literacy Understanding and Responding to Texts: Ages 9–10*). Groups should use this to record detailed information about each activity to help them to plan a documentary for video recording.

A Lesson for Every Day
Literacy
9–10 Years
© A&C Black

On screen: 1

- **Plan a short play to introduce your documentary about leisure activities.**
- **Begin with two bored children.**
- **Then bring in their parents.**

Work in a group.

What might the bored children say?

What might their parents say?

Think about facial expressions.

Think about actions and body language.

List of characters

Name	Description	Name	Description

Dialogue

Speaker	Stage directions	Spoken words

NOW TRY THIS!

- **Act the play with someone watching.**
- **Edit the script.**

How does it look and sound to the audience?

Teachers' note The children should first have completed pages 'Leisure survey' and 'Leisure documentary planner'. They can then work in groups to write the script for a mini-play as an introduction to their documentary. They could first enact a scenario in which some bored children are complaining about having nothing to do or are in trouble for anti-social behaviour which they say arose through boredom. Continued on 'On screen: 2'.

A Lesson for Every Day
Literacy
9-10 Years
© A&C Black

121

On screen: 2

- **Link the** play **to the** documentary **that will follow it.**

> Think about what the play was saying and what you found out for your documentary.

One of the characters could speak to camera.
- **What could he or she say?**

Scene location _____

Character	On screen Will the character be with the others from the play? Will he or she move away from them? How can you make the others 'disappear'?	Spoken words

Then a reporter could come on screen to introduce the documentary.

> Change the background setting to introduce the leisure activities.

Scene location at start _____

Changes in background/location _____

Reporter	On screen Will the reporter stand still or walk towards something or someone?	Spoken words

NOW TRY THIS!

- **Video your introduction.**
- **Play it and make** notes **about how to improve it.**

Teachers' note The children should first have completed the activities on 'Leisure survey' and 'Leisure documentary planner'. They could take turns to video record their first attempt and then replay it and edit it to produce a polished performance. They can then plan the factual part of the documentary, with different groups collaborating to produce a report about different types of activity.

A Lesson for Every Day
Literacy
9-10 Years
© A&C Black

Sentence combinations

- **Read each set of sentences.**
- **Write the same information in one sentence.**

The word-bank will help.

You can miss out some words.

You can change some words.

You can change the order of the words.

1 That is my friend. He won the front crawl race.
His name is William.

  <u>That is my friend William, who won the front crawl race.</u>

2 She lost a five-pound note. She had already lost another one.

  <u>Having lost</u> _____

  _____

3 Henry VIII was born in 1491. He died in 1547. He ruled England from 1509 to 1547.

  _____

  _____

4 He cannot sing. He cannot dance. He can play the piano brilliantly.

  _____

  _____

5 I play tennis. I play football. I can't skate.

  _____

  _____

NOW TRY THIS!

- **Write three short sentences about someone from the past.**
- **Write the same information in one sentence.**

Teachers' note Read the first example with the children and point out that in some texts short sentences work well but others can be improved by joining sentences which give pieces of information that are connected. Explain that words such as *who*, *when*, *where*, *which* and *that* are useful, as are punctuation marks such as commas, semi-colons, colons, dashes and brackets.

A Lesson for Every Day
Literacy
9–10 Years
© A&C Black

123

Two talks: 1

1 "Ladies and gentlemen – it gives me great pleasure to welcome you to the eighty-fourth annual Upper Snobbleby Summer Fair. I am delighted to see so many visitors from farther afield in addition to the usual wonderful turn-out of villagers old and young.

The proceeds will be donated to the village hall repair fund. The village hall is a vital part of our community, being the venue for our Guides, Scouts, the Women's Institute, fitness classes and musical groups.

This year visitors can win prizes from stalls such as the coconut shy, roll-a-pound, tombola and donkey derby. In addition to these there are several food-stalls selling home-grown produce, home-baked cakes and bread and home-made preserves.

Visitors are reminded to submit entries for the horticultural and cooking competitions and the dog show, all of which have separate sections for children under the age of fifteen.

Refreshment can be found in the marquee, where tea, coffee and other beverages, sandwiches, savouries and home-baked cakes and biscuits can be purchased.

Without more ado, I hereby declare the eighty-fourth Upper Snobbleby Fair open."

2 "Hi, guys. Great to see you all here at Tupfield. We're gonna have a great time today and raise loadsa funds for the village while we're at it. All the ticket money goes straight to the fund to tidy up the green and the pond and buy benches, an' now there's six chaps comin' round with raffle tickets. 25p each an' you can win any of these prizes here: a plasma telly, a DAB radio, this nice rug, a table lamp, a big shopping bag full of food or a voucher for lunch for two at the village caff. So don't forget to buy your ticket.

Have a go at paintball or crazy golf. Guess the weight of the chicken. Ride in a tractor. Have a photo taken as a Roman soldier. Go on – don't be shy.

I hope you've brought your dog for the dog show – starts at twelve. And your pets for the kids' pets competition in the corner over there, at two.

They're taking entries now for the baking competition and the gardening – over there in the long tent. Kids under fifteen have a special section – so you're all in with a chance.

An' if you're feelin' peckish just take a stroll along to the big tent and see what wonderful grub they've got: pies, cakes, biscuits, baps, tea, coffee and all kinds of cold drinks. There's the chip van as well, and the ice cream van.

Well – that's all from me, folks. Enjoy your day."

Teachers' note Ask the children to think about the different ways in which they speak to different people. They are probably more likely to use slang when speaking to people they know well. Remind them that slang does not necessarily mean swear-words and that they are banned from this activity.

A Lesson for Every Day
Literacy
9–10 Years
© A&C Black

Two talks: 2

- **Look for examples of each language feature in the two talks.**

Work with a group.

Language features	Examples	
	Talk 1	**Talk 2**
Use of the first person		
Use of the second person		
Use of the third person		
Mainly active verbs		
Mainly passive verbs		
Use of the instruction form of verbs		
Long sentences		
Short sentences		
Contractions		
Slang		
Formal words		
Informal words		

NOW TRY THIS!

- **Write a paragraph to say how you recognise formal and informal language.**

Teachers' note Ask the children to think about the different ways in which they speak to different people. They are probably more likely to use slang when speaking to people they know well. Remind them that slang does not necessarily mean swear-words and that they are banned from this activity.

A Lesson for Every Day
Literacy
9–10 Years
© A&C Black

Instruct me

- **Read the** recount **that tells how someone used a computer program**
- **Rewrite it as** instructions **to tell someone how to use the program.**

I put the CD-ROM *Ponds and Streams* into the CD-ROM drive.
When it had loaded, I waited for it to finish the introduction.
Then I clicked on 'Visit the pond'. This started a pond game.
I had to explore the pond and complete all the tasks the pond animals gave me.
I clicked on 'Start new game'. I keyed in my name and clicked OK. A pond came on the screen.
I moved the cursor around the edges of the screen. If an arrow showed, I clicked on it to move right, left, up or down around the pond.
When an animal appeared I clicked on it. This displayed an information box about the animal.
To get rid of the box I clicked on it.
Sometimes a box appeared that gave me a task to complete.
After I had read these I had to click OK to get rid of them.
Each time I completed a task I scored points.
I could end the game at any time by clicking 'End game'.

How to Play the Pond Game

1   Put the CD-ROM 'Ponds and Streams' into the CD-ROM drive.

2   When it has loaded,

3   _____

4   _____

5   _____

6   _____

7   _____

8   _____

9   _____

10 _____

NOW TRY THIS!

- **What else would you like to know?**
- **Write three questions.**

Teachers' note Copy this onto A3 paper. Ask the children to read the passage and to identify the features that show it is a recount (past tense, written in the order in which events happened, time connectives such as *Then*). Ask them which words they will change, and how, in order to convert it into instructions. For a more challenging activity the completed example could be masked.

A Lesson for Every Day
Literacy
9-10 Years
© A&C Black

Mixed-up instructions

- **Write** instructions **for the Pond Game tasks. The children's recounts are not in the correct order, so you will need to sort them out.**

We did this by dragging each bit of litter we found into the backpack. We cleared the litter from the pond. We found the backpack at the bottom left of the screen.

We had to continue until she was covered. We did this by dragging bits and pieces such as leaves and sticks onto her. We helped Kitty Caddis to make a new case.

We clicked on each pond animal to find out which one had the lens. First we looked around the pond until we heard the Cyclops say Hello. Once we had found the lens we dragged it onto the backpack icon and clicked on the lens. Then we could see the Cyclops. The Cyclops was too small to see so we had to look for an old spectacle lens to help.

Clear the pond of litter

_____

_____

Help Kitty Caddis to make a new case

_____

_____

_____

Look for the Cyclops

_____

_____

_____

_____

_____

NOW TRY THIS!

- **List any words you think should be in the** glossary .
- **Write** definitions **for them.**

Teachers' note Each speech bubble presents a recount of a task within the Pond Game. The children need not have used the software, since the focus is on the language and structure of instructions. Ask them to identify the sentence that should come first in each recount. They should notice that the other sentences do not make sense unless they follow this 'topic sentence'.

A Lesson for Every Day
Literacy
9-10 Years
© A&C Black

The instructor

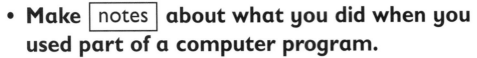

- Make notes about what you did when you used part of a computer program.

> You could number each note to help.

- Check that your notes are in the correct order.
- Use your notes to help you to write instructions.

Instructions

Name of program _____

Name of the part used _____

Purpose _____

1 _____

2 _____

3 _____

4 _____

5 _____

6 _____

NOW TRY THIS!

- Give your instructions to a friend to test and edit.

Teachers' note Use this with any suitable software with which the children are familiar. They should focus on an activity within the program and make notes about how they used it. They can then fill out their notes as instructions to tell someone what to do, rather than as a recount of what they did.

A Lesson for Every Day
Literacy
9–10 Years
© A&C Black

Formal or informal

Rewrite these ▢formal sentences as ▢informal sentences.

Guests are requested not to deposit their broomsticks or wands in the vestibule.	<u>Please don't leave</u> _____ _____ _____
The restaurant wishes to remind diners that owls are not permitted in this establishment.	<u>No owls</u> _____ _____ _____
The preparation and application of magical concoctions are forbidden on these premises.	<u>Please don't</u> _____ _____ _____
Spectators are reminded that attendance at a game of quidditch is at their sole risk.	<u>You watch</u> _____ _____ _____
Phillipa Jane Sands hereby bequeaths the sum of 300 galleons to her son Phillip, unless he predeceases her.	<u>Pip is leaving 300</u> _____ _____ _____

NOW TRY THIS!

• **Write a formal and an informal sentence telling people at a football match that they must not stand on their seats.**

eachers' note Demonstrate the difference between formal and informal texts by looking at ormation leaflets and chatty notes. Ask the children which style they would use for writing a note a friend and which they would use for writing a letter to someone they do not know. Ask them to scribe the differences between the two styles.

A Lesson for Every Day
Literacy
9–10 Years
© A&C Black

A closer look

What are the differences between formal **and** informal **writing?**

- Compare the examples.
- Write your answers on the chart.

Use a ✔

Formal

Mr & Mrs William Arramee request
the pleasure of the company of

Mrs Flora Getty

at the marriage of their daughter Bridie
to Mr Paul Groom.

A deposit of £5 is required for the
hire of sports equipment. This will
be refunded on the return of
equipment in good order.

Informal

Flo – we've asked a few friends over on Sat (about 7pm), can you come? Hope so. Talk soon. Hugs and xx   Bill

There's a deposit of £5 when you hire sports gear. Bring it back undamaged and you get your £5 back.

Features	Formal				Informal			
	many	some	a few	none	many	some	a few	none
Passive verbs								
Contractions: e.g. I'm								
Non-standard English								
Everyday words								
Difficult/long words								
First person								
Second person								
Third person								

NOW TRY THIS!

- **List three purposes for these:**

formal writing   informal writing

Teachers' note Ask the children to read the passages and to notice the differences between the formal and informal ones. Discuss the audience and purpose of each one and why a formal or informal style is suitable. Before the children start writing, they could 'act out' the formality/informality with a partner (for example, putting on a 'posh' voice).

A Lesson for Every Day
Literacy
9–10 Years
© A&C Black

Instruction sentences

Change the sentences into | instructions | .

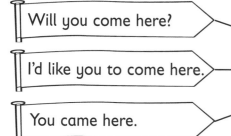

Will you come here?

I'd like you to come here.

You came here.

→ Come here.

---

1 Can you hop along this line?

_____

6 You closed the gate.

_____

2 You posted the letter.

_____

7 Did you lock the door?

_____

3 You turned left.

_____

8 Are you going home?

_____

4 Did you mix the eggs and sugar?

_____

9 You did not touch the stove.

_____

5 I'd like you to make me a cup of tea.

_____

10 You go to school.

_____

NOW TRY THIS!

- **Circle the verbs in each sentence.**
What do you notice about the positions of the verbs?
What else do you notice about the verbs?

chers' note Read the completed example with the children and ask them which sentence gives
instruction. Discuss how to recognise an instruction sentence: it begins with a verb in the present
se and does not need a noun or pronoun; it ends with a full stop.

A Lesson for Every Day
Literacy
9–10 Years
© A&C Black

Recount to instruction

- **Read the** [recount] .
- **Write** [instructions] **for making friends.**

How I made friends

I asked to join in games. I said Hello to people. I listened to people. I smiled. I helped others. I shared things. I comforted people who were hurt or upset. I learned some jokes to tell. I laughed when others told jokes. I tried to be fair. If anyone was alone I invited them to join in my group.

Instructions
How to make friends

_____

_____

_____

_____

_____

_____

_____

_____

NOW TRY THIS!

- **Write three instruction sentences on how to deal with bullies.**
- **Share your ideas with a partner.**

Teachers' note Tell the children that they are going to read a recount about what someone did in order to make friends. Ask them how the sentences in a recount are different from instructions. Draw out that they are written for a different purpose (to tell what happened, rather than to tell someone what to do), they are in the past tense and they do not begin with a verb.

A Lesson for Every Day
Literacy
9–10 Years
© **A&C Black**

Make it work!

- Write instructions for finding out what is wrong if a circuit does not work.

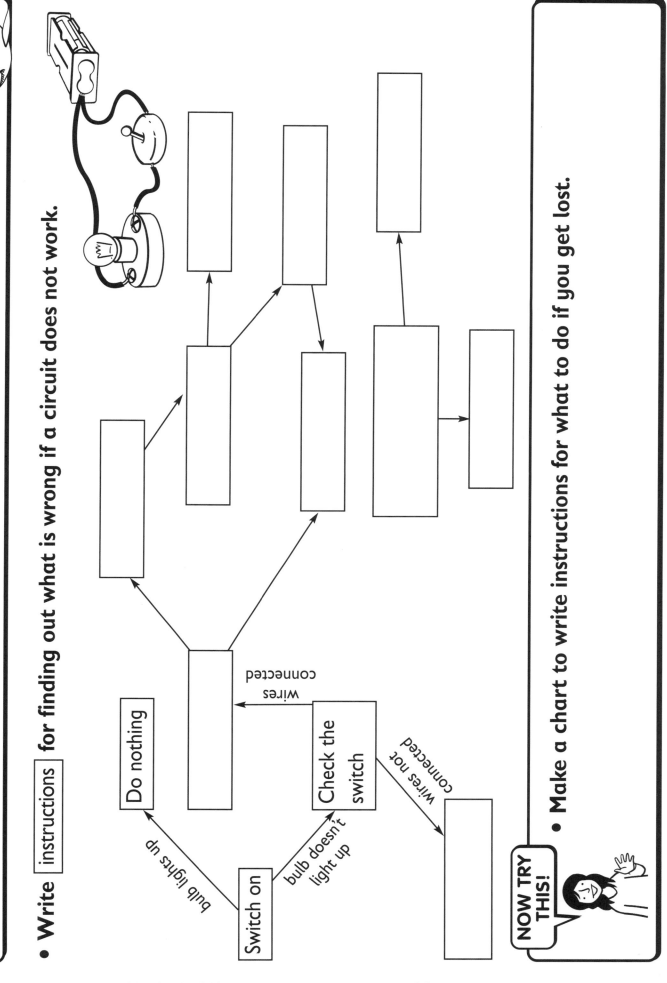

Do nothing

wires connected

Switch on

Check the switch

bulb lights up

bulb doesn't light up

wires not connected

NOW TRY THIS!

- Make a chart to write instructions for what to do if you get lost.

achers' note Copy this page onto A3 so that the children have more space for their answers. Tell
em that the flow-chart can be used to help to plan instructions which change depending on what
ppens: if the light comes on when the switch is switched on the reader need not do anything, but if
e light does not come on he or she needs to check each part of the circuit.

A Lesson for Every Day
Literacy
9-10 Years
© A&C Black

Making it clear

- **Write the two possible meanings of these sentences.**
- **Rewrite the sentences so that their correct meaning is clear.**

The bag was found by a police officer hidden in the washing machine.

Meaning 1 _____

Meaning 2 _____

Correct _____

Mrs Bell was looking for a car in part exchange for her husband.

Meaning 1 _____

Meaning 2 _____

Correct _____

If your dog likes liver, cover it and braise it in a moderate oven.

Meaning 1 _____

Meaning 2 _____

Correct _____

NOW TRY THIS!

- **Explain how you changed each sentence to make it clear.**

Think about ...

... the order of words and phrases ...

... pronouns

... punctuation

Teachers' note Read the first sentence with the children and ask them what it means. Then ask them what else it could mean. Which is the more likely meaning? Discuss how to make this meaning clear – in this case by altering the order of the phrases (*hidden in the washing machine* should precede *by a police officer*).

A Lesson for Every Day
Literacy
9–10 Years
© A&C Black

Slang match

- **What would you say if you used slang words instead of these?**
- **Write a sentence using each slang word.**

Hi, Missus!

Slang does not mean swear-words.

Standard English	Slang	Sentence
a large amount		
difficult		
dreadful		
excellent		
food		
get/do something wrong		
money		
problem or trouble		
relax		
scared		
steal		

NOW TRY THIS!

- **Talk to a partner about when, where and with whom you would use slang words.**
- **List some situations where you would not use slang.**

eachers' note Ask the children to think about the different ways in which they speak to different ople. They are probably more likely to use slang when speaking to people they know well. Remind em that slang does not necessarily mean swear-words and that they are banned from this activity.

A Lesson for Every Day
Literacy
9-10 Years
© A&C Black

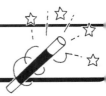

Speech: formal or informal

• **Write a more suitable answer for each question.**

Well done. What are you going to do to relax?

Thanks, missus. I'm off with me missus and the kids to chill out in Mexico.

_____
_____
_____

What exactly were you doing on the level crossing?

Er .. I were just 'avin' a chat, like, wiv our Donna an' 'er mate when the bizzies clocked us.

_____
_____
_____

How did the shop window get broken?

I dunno, mate. It was broke when I got here. I never saw nuffin'.

_____
_____
_____

What do you think about winning a gold medal?

Wicked! I was gobsmacked but I'm well chuffed.

_____
_____
_____

NOW TRY THIS!

• **Continue one of the conversations and role-play it with a partner in informal and then formal language.**

Teachers' note Discuss what is meant by formal and informal language: formal speech is usually used with people the children do not know well, older people or people in positions of authority. It does not include slang or dialect words. Formal language is used on special occasions such as ceremonies, serious meetings and so on.

A Lesson for Every Day
Literacy
9–10 Years
© A&C Black

Question time

- **Answer the questions.**
- **Write the answers on the cards.**
- **Then sort the questions into two sets:** | open | **and** | closed |.

What is your favourite colour?	Do you like dogs?
What would your perfect school be like?	How do you choose your friends?
What time do you go to bed?	Have you read *Harry Potter and the Deathly Hallows*?
What sorts of book do you like to read?	Do you have a television in your bedroom?
Did you have breakfast today?	What do you think of the idea of splitting the school year into four terms?
Do you prefer to swim in salt or fresh water?	What do you think makes a place good for holidays?

NOW TRY THIS!

- **Write four open questions you could ask someone you want to make friends with.**

Teachers' note Explain that the response to a closed question is usually short: for example, a number, yes or no. An open question usually invites a fuller answer such as an opinion, an explanation. You could demonstrate by asking the children some open and closed questions.

A Lesson for Every Day
Literacy
9–10 Years
© A&C Black

Interview improver

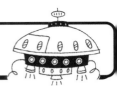

- **Role-play the interview with a partner.**
- **Then discuss how the questions can be improved.**

Work in a group of four to six.

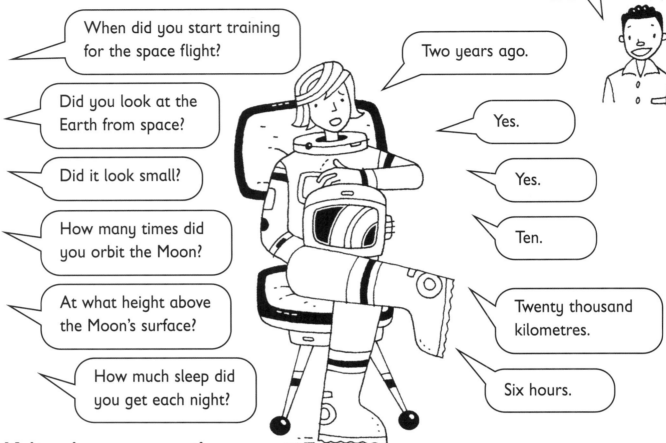

When did you start training for the space flight?

Two years ago.

Did you look at the Earth from space?

Yes.

Did it look small?

Yes.

How many times did you orbit the Moon?

Ten.

At what height above the Moon's surface?

Twenty thousand kilometres.

How much sleep did you get each night?

Six hours.

- **Write six new questions.**

1 _____

2 _____

3 _____

4 _____

5 _____

6 _____

NOW TRY THIS!

- **Choose two people to role-play the interview using the new questions.**
- **Discuss how the answers are different, and why.**

Teachers' note The children should work in a group large enough to provide role-players and an audience and decide among themselves who should do what. The audience should identify the types of question asked; the group can then discuss how interesting the answers were and how to ask questions that produce more information or ideas.

A Lesson for Every Day
Literacy
9–10 Years
© A&C Black

Leading questions

- **Underline the leading questions in this interview.**
- **Choose three leading questions and explain why they were hard to answer.**

Work with a partner.

Interviewer: Is it fair that your buying power means small stores can't compete on prices?

Supermarket manager: We give customers great deals.

Interviewer: You haven't answered the question about fairness.

Supermarket manager: Competition is good for the customer.

Interviewer: Well, I can see that you are not going to answer my question about fairness. What about the traffic problems your store has caused since it opened?

Supermarket manager: We have provided a large car park.

Interviewer: How do you answer local people's complaints about vehicles queuing up in front of their homes waiting to get into your car park?

Supermarket manager: We're offering them a great local shopping facility with good parking.

Interviewer: Would you like cars in front of your house all day and night?

Supermarket manager: The queues only happen at very busy times and I'd like to point out…

Interviewer: Yes, but would you like it?

Supermarket manager: Well, of course not but …

Interviewer: I'm glad we can agree that you have caused traffic chaos here and forced the closure of many small local shops.

Leading question	Wanted answer	What made the question difficult to answer
Is it fair that your buying power means small stores can't compete on prices?	No	'Yes' looks as if the supermarket doesn't care about small stores. 'No' suggests that it knowingly acts unfairly.

NOW TRY THIS!

- **Rewrite the interviewer's questions, making them fairer.**
- **Role-play the new interview.**

Teachers' note Introduce the term leading question and use examples to model some leading questions (see notes on the activity page 18). Ask the children how these questions influence the answer and how to ask a fairer question. You could also discuss who might ask leading questions, and why.

A Lesson for Every Day
Literacy
9–10 Years
© A&C Black

Rhetorical questions

- ## Try answering the questions.
- ## What do you notice?

 Work with a partner.

 How many times must I tell you – NO!

 Three thousand seven hundred and twenty-two!

 Don't be cheeky.

 How would you like it if you had to tidy up after everyone?

What's the point of having a bike if I'm never allowed to go anywhere on it?

Why should we put up with his bad temper?

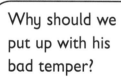  

When is it going to stop raining?

NOW TRY THIS!

- ## Write four rhetorical questions with your partner.
- ## Discuss why they are used.
- ## Share your answer with another pair.

Teachers' note You could model some rhetorical questions and introduce this term. Ask the children how they might reply to them and draw out that when people ask rhetorical questions they do not expect an answer but use them for emphasis or to express emotions or opinions.

A Lesson for Every Day
Literacy
9–10 Years
© A&C Black

Word match game

- **Choose a speech bubble.**
- **Say the word to the person next to you.**
- **They should say an informal word or words that mean the same.**

Play in a group. Take turns clockwise.

Example:

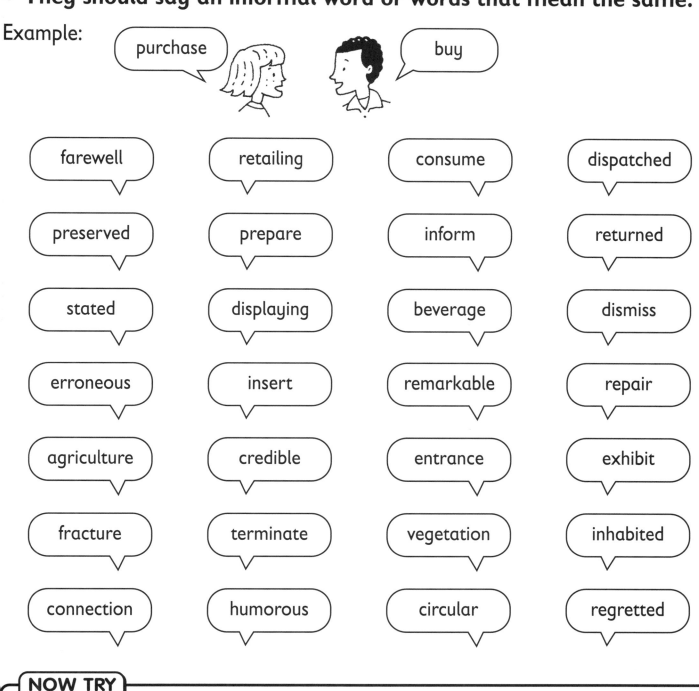

purchase

buy

farewell	retailing	consume	dispatched
preserved	prepare	inform	returned
stated	displaying	beverage	dismiss
erroneous	insert	remarkable	repair
agriculture	credible	entrance	exhibit
fracture	terminate	vegetation	inhabited
connection	humorous	circular	regretted

NOW TRY THIS!

- **Tell your group the formal word for two of these:**

baby   clap   choose   extra   fun   get
help   lift   make   quick   real   see   stop

Use a thesaurus.

Teachers' note The children should first have had opportunities to read and listen to formal and informal language. You could also compare some of the vocabulary in the two talks on 'Two talks: 2'. After they have completed the page they could consider who might use each example, with what kind of audience and in what context.

A Lesson for Every Day
Literacy
9–10 Years
© A&C Black

Older people: 1

- **Sort the cards:** | true | | false | | not sure |

'Older' means over the age of 60.	Older people need help filling in forms and dealing with bills.	No older people are alone nowadays because health workers visit them.
There are older people in our community who need help in looking after themselves: bathing, dressing and so on.	There are no older people in our area who are poor.	'Poor' means not being able to afford new clothes.
'Poor' means not being able to afford enough to eat, or to keep your home warm enough.	All older people should have a television set.	There are older people in our community who cannot afford to keep warm in the winter.
Some older people in our area need help with shopping.	Transport is difficult for older people.	Some older people in our area would like more company.
Our local community has enough clubs and other activities for older people.	There are organisations in our area that can help older people in every way they need.	The local council provides everything that older people need.
Older people do not want others doing things for them.	Some older people in our area would like help with keeping their gardens tidy.	Some older people in our area would like help in getting to activities that are not specially for older people, but for anyone.
Older people do not like having children around them.	Some older people in our local community need help with housework.	All older people in our local community need help with housework.

Teachers' note Ask the children to read each card as a group and to decide in which set it belongs. If the whole class is working on this they could then move around the room to look at the ways in which other groups have sorted the cards and make a note of any differences from their own. These could be discussed in the plenary and lead to researching the topic (see 'Older people: 2 and 3').

A Lesson for Every Day
Literacy
9–10 Years
© A&C Black

Older people: 2

- **What can you do to help older people in your local community?**
- **Plan a survey to find out about one of the following:**

  a) meals   b) housework   c) shopping   d) transport

  e) activities   f) form-filling, bills and letters

The topic we are researching is _____

- **Decide where to find each piece of information and who will find it.**

Work in a group.

Find out about what help older people get, who helps and what else they would like.

The help older people already get	Who provides the help	How useful this is

- **What other help would older people like, and why?**

_____

_____

_____

NOW TRY THIS!

- **Talk together about anything you can do to help.**

You might be able to do things yourselves, find others who can help or raise money to pay for help.

Teachers' note The children should first have completed 'Older people: 1'. The topics arising from this should be distributed among the class for different groups to research. You will need to plan how the research can be carried out, with the support of other adults where off-site visits are required.

A Lesson for Every Day
Literacy
9–10 Years
© A&C Black

Older people: 3

- **How are you going to help older people in your local community?**

Work in a group.

You should first have done a survey to find out what is needed.

_____

- **List everything you will need to do:**

_____   _____

_____   _____

_____   _____

- **List any equipment you will need:**

_____   _____

_____   _____

_____   _____

- **What help will you need from teachers or other adults?**

_____

_____

_____

- **Talk together about who will be responsible for organising each task.**

Task	Who will be responsible

NOW TRY THIS!

- **Present your plan to your teacher and your class.**
- **Make notes about anything you will need to change.**

Others might come up with better ideas. Listen and think.

Teachers' note The children should first have completed 'Older people: 1 and 2'. Ask them how their ideas about what older people in the community wanted or needed and what is available compared with the facts they found out. Different groups could work on different aspects of helping older people in the community. Remind them of the importance of listening to the ideas of the group.

A Lesson for Every Day
Literacy
9-10 Years
© A&C Black

What's my role?

- **What role did these children take in their group discussions?**
- **What else could they have done in this role?**
- **Write on the notes.**

I asked the group for their views.

Role:

I took notes on the discussion.

Role:

I encouraged someone who is very quiet.

Role:

I told another group what we decided, and why.

Role:

NOW TRY THIS!

- **Share your ideas with a partner.**

Teachers' note It helps if the children have first completed page 143. They might find that the roles of leader and mentor overlap; to help them you could emphasise the supporting role of the mentor and refer back to their previous work on group leadership (page 109) to clarify that role.

A Lesson for Every Day
Literacy
9–10 Years
© A&C Black

Group chaos: 1

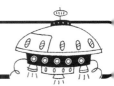

These children are deciding what to buy for Mrs Taylor, the school cook, for a retirement present.

- **What do they need to find out before they begin their discussion?**
- **Write in the boxes.**

A tree for her garden. Trees are good. It would make her garden nice and shady. Get a tree.

Leah

Zul

No – not a tree. A book. She'll have lots of time for reading when she retires.

_____

_____

_____

_____

_____

_____

Get some tickets for the pantomime. *The Sleeping Beauty* is on at the Empire. It's really funny. I went to see it with my mum so I know.

Amy

William

NO! The best thing to buy for her is a pair of gloves and a scarf. I saw her coming to school with no gloves or scarf on and she looked cold. Let's get her something sensible.

_____

_____

_____

_____

_____

_____

NOW TRY THIS!

- **What should the group do when they next have a discussion about the present?**

Teachers' note Ask the children to read the statements on this page and to think about how to choose a gift for 'Mrs Taylor'. They should make notes about what each child depicted here should find out in order to justify his or her choice of gift. They could also use this page to help them to choose a real gift for someone they know (just edit it using the CD-ROM).

A Lesson for Every Day
Literacy
9-10 Years
© **A&C Black**

Group chaos: 2

This is what the children found out.
- **What should the group leader ask each of them?**
- **Write the questions.**
- **Make up an answer for each question.**
- **Then write the group leader's summary of all the suggestions. Use a separate sheet of paper.**

Leah

> The garden centre has wild cherry trees 250 cm high for £15.

Zul

> Mrs Taylor likes cooking. We could buy 'Jamie at Home' – Jamie Oliver's book.

Amy

> It costs £20 for an adult to go to 'Sleeping Beauty' in the best seats.

William

> I saw lots of gloves and scarves in Marcus and Spectres when I went with my mum.

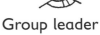

Group leader

NOW TRY THIS!

- **What should the group do next?**

Teachers' note The children should first have completed 'Group chaos: 1'. Ask them to read the facts those children found out to support their choice of gift. Remind them of the role of the group leader in ensuring that the group has all the information it needs to make a decision and the types of question he or she needs to ask. Here the leader needs to ask for more information from each member.

A Lesson for Every Day
Literacy
9–10 Years
© A&C Black

Word-maker

- **Make as many different words as you can using a prefix and a base word, or a base word and a suffix, or all three together.**
- **List the words.**

Prefixes

a   com   con

de   dis   ex   im

in   ir   non

re   un

Base words

accept   access

achieve   act   agree

avail   change   code

confide   differ   duct

obey   open   part   ply

press   ration   regular

sense   shame   wake

Suffixes

able   al   ance

ed   en   ence   ent

ful   ible   ical

ing   ion   ity

ment   or   ure

reaction

_____

NOW TRY THIS!

- **Make four words that have two prefixes and a suffix or a prefix and two suffixes.**

Teachers' note Demonstrate how to approach this activity by 'thinking aloud'– trying each prefix in turn with accept and, when none makes a word, saying *Perhaps a suffix will work: acceptable – yes – that's a word … I can add 'un' now – 'unacceptable'. I'll try the other suffixes … accepted … Yes, that's a word … acceptance … that's another. I wonder if I can add a prefix to these …*

A Lesson for Every Day
Literacy
9–10 Years
© A&C Black

The prefix a

Complete each sentence with a word from the word-bank with the prefix a added.
The new word should mean the same as the word or words in brackets.

Word-bank

blaze   board   company   part
range   rise   ~~sleep~~   sorted

You might need to double the first letter of the base word.

Late last night, while we were <u>asleep</u> in our beds, someone broke into the house. (dozing)

We bought a bag of _____ sweets to put in the party goody bags. (mixed)

Richard asked Danayal if he would _____ him to the football match. (go with)

We dialled 999 and asked for the fire brigade when we saw the house _____. (burning)

In a poetic speech the army leader said, "I shall _____ and lead you all to victory." (get up)

The puppy pulled the cushion _____. (into pieces)

The boat set out to sea once all the passengers were _____. (on the boat)

The caretaker said he would _____ the tables in the hall. (set out)

NOW TRY THIS!

• Use the prefix a to form the words that have the opposite meaning to these.

descend   detach   decelerate

Use a thesaurus or a dictionary of synonyms and antonyms.

achers' note Ask the children for a word similar to sleep that means sleeping (asleep). What prefix d they add to the base word? Ask them to make a word in a similar way from wake (awake). Then k them how they can change the word count to mean a bill for payment (account). Discuss how this as different from the other two examples (the c at the beginning of count was doubled).

A Lesson for Every Day
Literacy
9-10 Years
© A&C Black

149

Word challenge

- In each row write words that begin with the prefix in the left-hand column.

You might need to change the spelling of the base word.

Use a dictionary.

Base word

Prefix	tract	tend	cord	pose
a				
com				
con				
de				
dis				
ex				
in				
re				

NOW TRY THIS!

- Write the meanings of six words from the chart.
- Use them in sentences.

Teachers' note After the children have completed the chart, ask different groups to write the meanings of different groups of words (for example, prefix a- and prefix com-; prefix con- and prefix de- and so on). Invite feedback and ask what the prefixes mean. Then ask them to check their answers in a dictionary.

150

A Lesson for Every Day
Literacy
9–10 Years
© A&C Black

Transfixed

- **Write a one-word** caption **for each picture. The word should have the prefix** trans .

You can see through glass.

I'll move this to another place.

I'll see if I can get this in English.

Les vacances en France

The boy who could change himself into an animal.

AMERICA
EUROPE
ATLANTIC OCEAN
AFRICA

Smith to move from Rangers to United

You can't see through the window but it lets light through.

TV CENTRE

NOW TRY THIS!

- **Think about the meanings of words that have the prefix** trans .
- **Use these to help you to decide what** trans **means.**
- **Check your answer in a dictionary.**

---

eachers' note The children could work in groups, discussing the meanings of the words in the word-ank, looking them up if necessary and matching them to the pictures.

A Lesson for Every Day
Literacy
9-10 Years
© A&C Black

Interaction

- **Play 'matching pairs'. Match the definitions to the words that have the prefix** inter .

international	interrupt	interpersonal	intercom
intercontinental	interlace	interval	intercity
intersect	interchange	interfere	interlocking
A station where passengers can change from one railway line to another or a place where many roads meet.	Between cities: for example a rail service between cities.	Short for intercommunication: a system for people to communicate by radio in a place such as an airport, hospital or school.	Between continents or connecting continents (for example, a railway or organisation).
To take part in something in a way that changes it in some way, usually without being invited.	To join two objects or ideas by binding them or tying them so that they are united.	Fitting together like a jigsaw puzzle.	Linking nations.
Linking people.	To butt into a conversation or other activity in a way that stops it.	To pass through or across something.	The time between two events or between parts of an event such as a film or play.

Teachers' note Ask the children to cut out the words with the prefix inter- (top half of the page) and their definitions (bottom half). They should mark the backs of one set. Spread both sets face down; the children take turns to turn over one of each, see if they match and either keep the pair or replace the cards. The winner is the player with the most pairs when no cards remain.

A Lesson for Every Day
Literacy
9-10 Years
© A&C Black

Word groups

- **Work in a group of four.**
- **Each choose a word from the box.**
- **Take turns to find a word in one of the ovals whose meaning is linked to your word.**
- **Explain the meaning to the group.**

Cross out each word in an oval after explaining the link.

medicament

mystify

employment

ploy

medicinal

gratuity

mysterious

employee

paramedic

employer

gratitude

medicine

mystic

medication

mystique

gratify

deploy

ungrateful

mystical

congratulate

NOW TRY THIS!

- **Write two words with meanings linked to each of these.**

nursery   herbivore   conifer

Teachers' note Explain that the spellings of many words can be learned by thinking of other words with similar spelling segments. Tell the children that all the words on this page can be put into just four groups.

A Lesson for Every Day
Literacy
9-10 Years
© A&C Black

153

Partners

- **Match each word in the sky to a word on a cloud.**
- **Write it on the cloud.**
- **Circle the similar** [letter strings] .
- **Tell a friend how the word on the cloud helps you to read its partner word.**

Look for similar spelling patterns.

pigeon

apostrophe

catalogue

leopard
_____

apostrophe
_____

coward
_____

mystique

miracle

marriage

carriage
_____

ferocious
_____

exhibition
_____

catastrophe   advantageous

mischief

hyphen
_____

certain
_____

jealous
_____

forward

jeopardy

hyacinth

chief
_____

obstacle
_____

dialogue
_____

atrocious

inhibition

courageous
_____

antique
_____

dungeon
_____

curtain

zealous

154

Teachers' note Point out that one way of learning how to spell difficult or irregular words is to think about other words with similar spelling patterns: for example, they might know *leopard* and when they come across *jeopardy* this will help them to read it.

A Lesson for Every Day
Literacy
9-10 Years
© A&C Black

Recount chronology: 1

Village Oak Mystery

'Old Tom' last summer.

Residents of Oakfield woke up this morning to find a huge gap where an ancient oak, known locally as 'Old Tom', used to stand.

During the night there had been gentle breezes but no strong winds and even if the tree had blown down it would surely be lying on its side on the green, but there was no trace of the tree. No roots remained in the ground, there were no stray twigs or leaves on the green and, said local residents, the old oak had been laden with acorns the day before but not a single acorn could now be seen on the green.

Oakfield resident Maria Greenstreet, 38, said, "I went out at midnight to look for my cat. He was stuck in the oak tree. I had to climb up and lift him out," adding that she had been wearing her nightdress and slippers.

But Cary Itoff, 25, said he thought he heard a heavy vehicle driving into the village and stopping. He and his band had been practising in his garage until the early hours of the morning. The others had left at about 4 am.

The *Daily Blab* managed to contact Gary Basher, 23, the band's drummer. "Oh, yes," he said. "At about 5 am I saw a huge gang of people sweeping the green by torchlight and piling rubbish into bags. There was a long articulated lorry parked right on the green. I didn't notice if the tree was still standing, but there were a lot of squirrels rushing about looking very agitated."

Lisa Lott, 57, said she was returning from a late shift at 5.30 am when she saw a large blue articulated lorry leaving Oakfield in the direction of Elmfield. She managed to read the sign on the side of the lorry as she passed it: 'George Oakley and Sons, timber suppliers'.

Police are investigating the matter. Inspector Justin Time said, "We have had reports of a large red lorry leaving Oakfield in the opposite direction to Elmfield at 5.20, with no sign on it," he said, "so people should not jump to the conclusion that Oakley's have stolen the tree." He added that a 57-year-old woman was helping the police with their enquiries.

Meanwhile Oakfield residents mourn the loss of their ancient oak. "There is an old saying that when Old Tom goes, Oakfield goes," said Jeremiah Sage, 107.

Teachers' note Remind the children of the structure of a recount: introduction, events recounted in a way that shows chorological order, summary paragraph. Reading in pairs, underline features such as *past tense verbs, time connectives* and *quotations*. Identify examples of direct speech (using speech bubbles) and reported speech (using expressions such as *said that*).

A Lesson for Every Day
Literacy
9–10 Years
© A&C Black

Recount chronology: 2

- **Write summaries of the** key events **in the** recount .
- **Cut out the boxes and glue them on the timeline in the order in which they happened.**

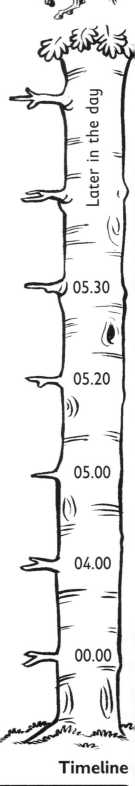

Later in the day

05.30

05.20

05.00

04.00

00.00

Timeline

Oak tree on green laden with acorns.

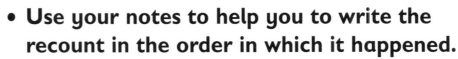

156

Teachers' note Use this with 'Recount chronology: 1'. The children could first cut the recount into separate paragraphs and arrange them in the order in which the events happened. Discuss why it was not written strictly in this order and how the writer indicated the order in which everything happened.

A Lesson for Every Day
Literacy
9–10 Years
© A&C Black

Recount features

- **Give examples of the features of** recounts **from** *Village Oak Mystery.*

Feature	Examples
Heading	
Introduction	
Past tense verbs	
Time connectives	
Quotations	
Reported speech	
Summary	
Indication of what might happen next	

NOW TRY THIS!

- **How is a recount different from an explanation?**
- **Plan an explanation of *Village Oak Mystery.***

Teachers' note Use this with 'Recount chronology: 1'. Ask the children to reread the recount and to look for the features listed on the chart. Ask them about the purpose of a recount (to tell a story in a way that shows the order in which events happened and how they were connected to one another).

A Lesson for Every Day
Literacy
9–10 Years
© A&C Black

157

Interviews to recount: 1

A reporter interviews people about a house fire that has just been put out.

Fire at 70 Hill Road, Whitehill

6 Feb

Good evening, Mrs Roe. I'm glad to see that you and baby Max are safe. When did you first notice the fire?

About 8 o'clock. I was in the kitchen and smelled smoke so I went in the hall. Smoke was coming under the lounge door. I ran up and grabbed the baby and ran outside.

When did you call the fire brigade?

Just after eight. I heard screaming and looked out and there was Emma running with the baby.

How do you think the fire started?

A lamp in the lounge was too near the curtains. That must have started it because that part of the room was the worst burned. The bulb got very hot and the curtains caught fire.

Was anyone hurt?

No. The neighbours were right to call an ambulance because they thought someone might still be in there. Mrs Roe's quick thinking saved the baby. If she'd opened the lounge door first, the fire would have got worse. She might not have been able to get upstairs to the baby. She could have been burnt.

Is the house safe?

We've checked and there's no serious damage, just one room burned and a lot of smoke damage. It's very wet from the fire hoses, too. It's not fit to sleep in tonight.

Where will you sleep tonight?

At my mum's round the corner. She said I can stay until the house is fixed.

Teachers' note Use this with 'Interviews to recount: 2'. Ask the children to read the interview notes to find out what happened and what people said about it. They can then use the newspaper writing format on page 159 to help them to write a recount about it.

A Lesson for Every Day
Literacy
9-10 Years
© A&C Black

Interviews to recount: 2

- **Write a** [newspaper recount] **about the house fire at 70 Hill Road.**
- **Use information from the** [interviews].
- **Include some** [quotations].

Headline _____

by _____

Introduction _____   _(Set the scene for the reader.)_

_____

Narrative _____   _(Say whose house caught fire and who lived there.)_

_____

Quotation _____   _(Quote the householder.)_

_____

Quotation _____   _(Quote the neighbour.)_

_____

Narrative and reported speech _____   _(Report what the firefighter said about the cause of the fire.)_

_____

_____

Quotation _____   _(Quote the ambulance driver.)_

_____

Narrative _____   _(Report what the firefighter said.)_

_____

Quotation _____   _(Quote Emma Roe.)_

_____

Conclusion _____   _(Add a comment.)_

_____

NOW TRY THIS!

- **Read your recount with a friend. Does it answer the questions Who? Where? What? When? How?**
- [Edit] **the recount.**

achers' note Use this with 'Interviews to recount: 1'. Discuss the features of news recounts: the
nse, person and type of language. The children should write notes in the past tense and include
uotations (some direct speech and some reported). Remind them that the introduction should engage
e readers' interest as well as set the scene. The headline should grab attention and say what the
ory is about.

A Lesson for Every Day
Literacy
9-10 Years
© A&C Black

News summary

- **Write a one-sentence** summary **of each** paragraph .

Give the main points but not the details.

Most of the northeast region had snow today. It is cold and it will become colder tonight. This cold weather will cause the snow to freeze and there will be icy road surfaces.

Roads in the northeast will be icy when the snow freezes.

Councillors have arranged to put up signs in the park to tell people to clean up after their dogs and that if they do not they will be fined up to £1,000. This is because many residents have complained about the mess.

Today Mrs Lavinia Lifetime celebrated her 100th birthday. She was born 100 years ago in Longton and lived there until she married her husband, Arthur. They went to live in Skelton. That was where Arthur worked.

For several months people living in houses close to Range Moor have been reporting that they have seen a large black cat-like animal. RSPCA officers said that they will check if it is a panther.

There was a robbery at Knox bank today. Two armed men with stocking masks over their heads rushed into the bank and forced staff to hand over all the cash. This came to more than £60,000.

Drivers had to wait for four hours while the police, fire brigade and council workers cleared the main road after a lorry overturned and its load of cartons of soup, cartons of orange juice and cartons of coleslaw spilled over the road.

NOW TRY THIS!

- **Write your sentences as news headlines.**
These need not be sentences.

ICE WARNING AS SNOW FREEZES

160

Teachers' note Tell the children that they are going to read some news items and to look for the main events. They could make a note of these on a piece of scrap paper before they write a sentence to summarise the news. Use the completed example to demonstrate how the order of the information can be changed.

A Lesson for Every Day
Literacy
9–10 Years
© A&C Black

Headline to sentence

• **Write the** headlines **as** sentences .

Think about tenses.

Hundreds of jellyfish on beach

PC IN DRAMATIC DASH TO SAVE FIVE-YEAR-OLD ON RAILWAY

_____

_____

Town's oldest shop to close – supermarket blamed

_____

ROTARY CLUB HANDS OVER £1500 FROM STREET COLLECTION TO HOSPICE

_____

High street traffic lights out of action

New swimming pool set to open tomorrow

_____

DOG STARVED – OWNER FINED

Bull escapes from market

Circus comes to town

_____

_____

NOW TRY THIS!

• **Choose a sentence above.**
• **Add as much extra information as possible to it.**

Check the punctuation.

Teachers' note Read the first headline with the children and ask them if it is a sentence. Ask them to make it into a sentence and to punctuate it. Invite a volunteer to write this up or key it in for the others to read. Ask the others which words have been added, and why. They could also proofread it to check that it makes sense and to check the spelling and punctuation.

A Lesson for Every Day
Literacy
9–10 Years
© A&C Black

161

Rose conversation

- **Work in a group of six.**
- **Each examine a different part of a rose.**
- **Write notes about what you say the rose is like.**

> Compare it with everyday things.

Flower (smell)	Petal (feel)

Stem (feel)	Edge of leaf (feel)

Thorn (feel) ⚠ Take care	Flat part of leaf (feel)

- **Write your conversation on a separate piece of paper. Start like this:**

_____ said, "The rose is _____."

"It is like _____ ," said _____

_____

NOW TRY THIS!

- **Check and edit the conversation you wrote.**
- **See if you can improve it.**
- **Write the changes in a different colour.**

162

Teachers' note Give each child a copy of this page and ask them to make notes of what each member of their group says. They can then write this as a dialogue.

A Lesson for Every Day
Literacy
9–10 Years
© A&C Black

Come out to play

Read some of the reasons why many children do not play outdoors.

The roads are too dangerous.

You can't trust people these days. Children are not safe if you can't see them.

We are always being told off by adults for making a noise.

We're not allowed to play football anywhere.

I can't play with my netball net because my next-door neighbour complains about the noise of the ball hitting the wall.

My neighbour keeps my ball if it goes in his garden.

With a partner, talk about four arguments *for* letting children play outdoors.

Write them on the toys.

NOW TRY THIS!

- **Plan an argument to present to a group of adults.**
- **Use persuasive words.**

Teachers' note This page could be completed individually or working with a partner. After reading the reasons against letting children play outdoors they could share the task of thinking up arguments for it.

A Lesson for Every Day
Literacy
9–10 Years
© A&C Black

Is that a fact?

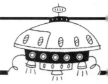

- **Sort the statements into two sets:**
  | facts | **and** | not facts | .

Which statements give true facts?

Which of these will persuade your audience?

Use information books and leaflets.

Use the Internet.

- **Choose three facts that you could use in an argument about whether people should eat meat.**

It is cruel to kill animals, so we should not eat them.	Meat causes cancer of the stomach, liver and intestines.
Meat contains protein. If we do not eat meat we will not get the protein we need for growth and for repairing the body.	We can get all the protein we need from plants: for example, lentils, beans, chickpeas, and from dairy foods such as cheese, milk and eggs.
People who do not eat meat develop anaemia. This means that they become weak because they do not have enough red blood cells.	Humans are animals. Many animals eat other animals.
If you eat only plant foods you will have fewer illnesses than people who eat meat.	You can stay healthy if you eat only plant foods but you have to be very careful.
You will not be clever if you do not eat meat.	People who eat meat get fat. Those who do not stay slim.

NOW TRY THIS!

- **Use the facts you chose to try to persuade someone who has the opposite view.**

Teachers' note The children could read the statements with a group and discuss whether they are true or whether they are not sure. The task of checking the ones they are not sure about could be shared between the group, with each child reporting back to the group at an agreed time. Emphasise that the 'facts' used in any argument should be accurate.

A Lesson for Every Day
Literacy
9-10 Years
© A&C Black

Sport at school: 1

Read what these children said about sport in their schools.

 Work in a group.

○ ○ ○
◀ ▶ ＋ | www.school_sport.com | Q

"Our school pays sports coaches to coach us for athletics after school but we have to pay to do it."

"We have two hours of PE, games and swimming lessons each week."

"As well as two hours of PE and sport each week, we have a breakfast-time club where we can play table tennis or tag-rugby."

"It takes ages to get to the swimming pool, then we have to wait until everyone is changed before we can get in. Some of them are really slow, so we never have long to swim."

"As well as our PE lessons we can choose all kinds of after-school clubs: such as dance, judo, tennis. It's great because I'm no good at the usual school stuff."

How would you like to improve sport at your school? Discuss the points you would like to make and write notes on the chart.

Sport at our school now	How we would like it to be

NOW TRY THIS!

- **Think of ways you could present the points you have made in a speech.**

eachers' note After reading the comments on the 'screen' the children could make statements about port at their school. Remind them of the need for accuracy when stating 'facts'. They can then discuss ny changes they would like to see, justifying their suggestions. Each group could appoint a reporter o report back to the class.

A Lesson for Every Day
Literacy
9-10 Years
© A&C Black

Sport at school: 2

- **Think about how you would like sports to be at your school.**
- **Plan your argument for this.**

> Decide on the best order for the points you make.

- **Introduce the topic.**

- **List the main suggestions you will make.**

Points I shall make	Information to support these points	Persuasive words and phrases to use
1		
2		
3		
4		
5		

- **Summarise your argument.**

NOW TRY THIS!
- **Present your argument to another group.**
- **Ask them what they thought was good about it.**

Teachers' note Copy this page onto A3 paper. The children should first have completed 'Sport at school: 1'. Ask them to think about the changes they would like to see in sport at their school. They should then think of how to present these in a way that might persuade their school council or headteacher.

A Lesson for Every Day
Literacy
9-10 Years
© A&C Black

And now the news ...

- **Watch a formal news report and an informal one.**
- **Make notes on the chart to show the differences.**
  Give examples from the news reports.

This morning a black and white cat was rescued from a tree in north Oxford . . .

Are you fed up with exams? Well, school children in Glasgow have found a great new way to revise.

	Formal news report	Informal news report
Does the speaker use gestures?		
Does the speaker make jokes?		
Does the speaker use the word 'you'?		
Is the tone of voice friendly?		
Is slang used?		
Are passive verbs used?		
Is the vocabulary complicated?		

NOW TRY THIS!

- **Work with a partner. List any other differences you noticed between the news reports.**
- **Discuss the audience and purpose of each news report.**

eachers' note Before the lesson, record a national television news report (formal) and a children's .ews report (informal). Talk through the questions on the chart, then play the recordings and ask the hildren to answer the questions, giving examples from the news reports.

A Lesson for Every Day
Literacy
9-10 Years
© A&C Black

167

I Have a Dream

I say to you today, my friends...
I still have a dream.
It is a dream deeply rooted in the American dream.
I have a dream
that one day this nation will rise up and live out the true meaning of its creed:
"We hold these truths to be self-evident that all men are created equal."

I have a dream
that one day on the red hills of Georgia
the sons of former slaves and the sons of former slave-owners
will be able to sit down together at the table of brotherhood.

I have a dream
that one day, even the state of Mississippi,
a state sweltering with the heat of injustice,
sweltering with the heat of oppression,
will be transformed into an oasis of freedom and justice.

I have a dream
that my four little children will one day live in a nation
where they will not be judged by the colour of their skin,
but by the content of their character.
I have a dream today!

I have a dream
that one day ... right here in Alabama, little black boys and black girls
will be able to join hands with little white boys and white girls as sisters and brothers.
I have a dream today!

I have a dream...
This is our hope.
This is the faith that I go back to the South with...

Let freedom ring...!,
Allow freedom to ring...!
from every mountainside...
from every peak...
from every village, and every hamlet...
we will be able to join hands and sing...
"Free at last, free at last; thank God Almighty, we are free at last."

Dr Martin Luther King, Jnr
from the speech made at the Civil Rights march on Washington DC, 1963

Teachers' note Use this with 'I have a dream: 2'. Read the extracts from the speech to the children. You could also let them listen to the entire speech on the Internet (see notes on the activity on page 21).

A Lesson for Every Day
Literacy
9–10 Years
© A&C Black

I have a dream: 2

- **Listen to the speech 'I have a dream' by Dr Martin Luther King.**
- **Talk together about what he said.**
- **Write a sentence to summarise his dream:**

_____

_____

- **Listen to the speech again and look at passages from it.**
- **List examples to show how Dr King persuaded his audience.**

Ideas

People being united	Equality

Devices

Evoking images of places	Repetition

NOW TRY THIS!

- **Talk together about what makes the verbs in the speech very powerful.**
- **List six powerful verbs.**

Teachers' note Use this with 'I have a dream: 1'. The children could work individually or in pairs to identify the persuasive language features. They will need a copy of 'I have a dream: 1' for reference. They could begin by underlining examples of each language feature, using different colours and making a key.

Come buy: 1

Morning and evening
Maids heard the goblins cry:
'Come buy, come buy:
Apples and quinces,
Lemons and oranges,
Plump unpecked cherries,
Melons and raspberries,
Bloom-down-cheeked peaches,
Swart-headed mulberries,
Wild free-born cranberries,
Crab-apples, dewberries,
Pineapples, blackberries,
Apricots, strawberries: –
All ripe together,
In summer weather, –
Morns that pass by,
Fair eves that fly;
Come buy, come buy:
Our grapes fresh from the vine,
Pomegranates full and fine,
Dates and sharp bullaces,
Rare pears and greengages,
Damsons and bilberries,
Taste them and try:
Currants and gooseberries,
Bright-fire-like barberries,
Figs to fill your mouth,
Citrons from the South,
Sweet to tongue and sound to eye;
Come buy, come buy.'

Evening by evening
Among the brookside rushes,
Laura bowed her head to hear,
Lizzie veiled her blushes:
Crouching close together
In the cooling weather,
With clasping arms and cautioning lips,
With tingling cheeks and finger tips.
'Lie close,' Laura said,
Pricking up her golden head:
'We must not look at goblin men,
We must not buy their fruits:
Who knows upon what soil they fed
Their hungry thirsty roots?'
'Come buy,' call the goblins
Hobbling down the glen.

'Oh!' cried Lizzie, 'Laura, Laura,
you should not peep at goblin men.'
Lizzie covered up her eyes,
Covered lest they should look;
Laura reared her glossy head,
And whispered like the restless brook:
'Look, Lizzie, look, Lizzie,
Down the glen tramp little men.
One hauls a basket,
One bears a plate,
One lugs a golden dish
Of many pounds' weight.
How fair the vine must grow
Whose grapes are so luscious;
How warm the wind must blow
Through those fruit bushes.'
'No,' said Lizzie: 'No, no, no;
Their offers should not charm us,
Their evil gifts would harm us.' …

Lizzie met her at the gate
Full of wise upbraidings:
'Dear, you should not stay so late,
Twilight is not good for maidens;
Should not loiter in the glen
In the haunts of goblin men.
Do you not remember Jeanie,
How she met them in the moonlight,
Took their gifts both choice and many,
Ate their fruits and wore their flowers
Plucked from bowers
Where summer ripens at all hours?
But ever in the noon light
She pined and pined away;
Sought them by night and day,
Found them no more, but dwindled and grew grey;
Then fell with the first snow,
While to this day no grass will grow
Where she lies low…

From *Goblin Market* by Christina Rossetti

Glossary

bullace – a type of plum
barberry – red oblong berry of the berberis shrub
swart – black

Teachers' note Use this with 'Come and buy: 2'. Before reading the poem to the children explain the words they might not know. You could also display these – perhaps on an interactive whiteboard. After listening to the poem the children could add any other words that needed explaining. Ask them how the goblins try to persuade the girls to come and buy their fruits and how Lizzie resists.

A Lesson for Every Day
Literacy
9–10 Years
© A&C Black

Come buy: 2

- **Listen to the poem *Goblin Market*.**
- **Talk together about how the goblins try to persuade the girls to buy their fruits.**
- **List examples of:**

You could first underline examples in the poem, using different colours.

language about the freshness of the fruits	colourful language	'mouth-watering' language

- **Talk together about how Lizzie tries to persuade Laura to keep away from the goblins.**
- **List examples of:**

right and wrong	health or staying safe	warnings

NOW TRY THIS!

- **Which lines show that Laura tried to resist the goblins before they persuaded her?**
- **Talk with a partner and make notes to report to your group.**

Teachers' note Use this with 'Come and buy: 1'. The children could work individually or in pairs to identify the persuasive language features. They will need a copy of 'Come and buy: 1' for reference. They could begin by underlining examples of each persuasive language feature, using different colours and making a key.

A Lesson for Every Day
Literacy
9–10 Years
© A&C Black

171

LIVERPOOL JOHN MOORES UNIVERSITY
LEARNING SERVICES

Persuaders

- Watch a television programme in which someone tries to persuade another to do something.

Work in a group.

- Who was being persuaded, to do what and who was the persuader? _____

_____

- Which of the following types of persuasion did they use?
- Write examples.

Making the action seem exciting	Suggesting that those who do it are special or better than those who don't	Making the other person feel silly for not doing it

- List some persuasive words they used.

Verbs in the 'command' form (for example, 'go on')	Other verbs	Adjectives

NOW TRY THIS!

- Talk together about what made it difficult for the TV character to resist the persuasion.

Teachers' note Before this activity you will need to record an extract from a television programme, such as a 'soap', in which someone tries to persuade another to do something (bad or good) – or you might be able to use a 'watch again' facility. Ask the children to notice what the persuader does and the types of language he or she uses. Afterwards they could list these with their groups.

A Lesson for Every Day
Literacy
9–10 Years
© A&C Black

Holiday hints

- **Work in a group. You are going to plan a talk about being responsible on holiday.**
- **Choose a chairperson to lead your discussions.**
- **Read the problems. Think of advice to holiday-makers to help solve each problem.**
- **Write your ideas on the chart.**

Problem	What to do
Many holiday resorts have water shortages.	Take a shower rather than a bath. Turn off taps properly.
Some holiday-makers waste electricity.	
People leave litter on beaches. This looks ugly and can be dangerous to wildlife.	
Cigarettes and campfires can cause forest fires.	
Wildlife is disturbed when people walk in places they are not supposed to.	
Some holiday souvenirs are made from animals which are endangered species.	
Local people sometimes complain that holiday-makers are noisy and rude.	

Plan how you will give your talk. Who will do what?

NOW TRY THIS!

- **Talk to another group about how you organised your discussions. What did the chairperson do? Did everyone join in and have their say?**

eachers' note Split the class into groups of up to six and give each group a copy of this page.
tart by asking the children where they have been on holiday, and whether they were aware of
ny problems caused by visitors (for example, in hot countries visitors may be asked to save water).
ncourage the children to think about the role of chairperson and why it is useful.

A Lesson for Every Day
Literacy
9–10 Years
© A&C Black

Listen carefully

- **Work in a group. Read this conversation.**

'Mum,' said Ranjit. 'You know that fantastic bike I'm saving up for? They've got one at the bike shop and it's on special offer. They'll take weekly payments – so that means I could have it right away and pay it from my pocket money. It's a chance to save money, really. But you have to sign these papers . . .'

'I'm not sure about that,' said Ranjit's mum. 'I don't approve of having things before you can pay for them. This will mean that you are in debt and we would end up paying for it if you couldn't. I'll have to talk to your dad . . .'

- **Discuss what Ranjit's dad should say. Choose a chairperson to lead your discussions.**
- **Listen to other people and make notes about their views.**

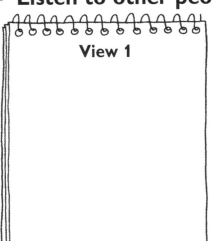

View 1

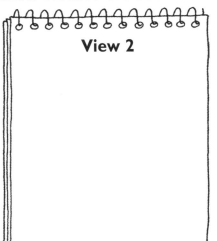

View 2

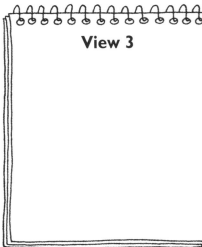

View 3

- **At the end of your discussion, the chairperson should sum up your group's views.**

NOW TRY THIS!

- **In your group, talk about how you organised your discussion. Was it a good idea to have a chairperson? Why?**

Would you do anything differently next time?

Teachers' note The children should work in groups of four. Give each child a copy of this page. Point out that the children may have different views, and everyone's opinions should be listened to and respected. Encourage the children to make notes about the different views expressed, including their own.

A Lesson for Every Day
Literacy
9-10 Years
© A&C Black

Shades of meaning

- **Work in a group. Cut out the cards.**
- **Match pairs of words that could mean the same thing.**
- **Look at each pair of words. Try to agree on how the meanings are different. Use the words in sentences to help explain your ideas.**

cowardly	enthusiast	fame
fanatic	fibs	persistent
flattery	foolhardiness	frown
harsh	heroism	lies
notoriety	obstinate	praise
sarcasm	scowl	skinny
spend	squander	stern
thin	timid	wit

NOW TRY THIS!

- **In each pair pair of words, one word suggests a more positive meaning than the other.**
- **Decide which word is more positive in each pair.**

achers' note Split the class into groups of four to six and give each group a copy of this page. sure that the children have access to a dictionary and thesaurus to check meanings. You may find it sier to allocate children with the task of finding out meanings before the group starts sorting.

A Lesson for Every Day
Literacy
9-10 Years
© A&C Black

Raise that cash

You are going to plan a charity fund-raising event.

- **Work in a group. Use this sheet to help you plan your event. You will need a chairperson and a scribe.**

Which charity will you choose?

Why?

What kind of event will you plan?

How will you raise money?

When and where will the event take place?

What will you need to do before the event? How will you share out the tasks?

What will you need to do during the event?

How long will it take to organise the event?

NOW TRY THIS!

- **Tell another group about your plans. Ask them if they think your idea will work.**
- **Think of ways to improve your plans. Make sure everyone agrees.**

Teachers' note Split the class into groups of up to six and give each group a copy of this page. Before the children begin the activity, discuss different charities and what they do. Remind them that the chairperson should be in charge of the discussion and make sure that everyone has their say. Encourage the children to achieve compromise where necessary.

A Lesson for Every Day
Literacy
9–10 Years
© A&C Black

A different bias: 1

• **Read these reports. Which report approves of 'trick or treat'?**

① Halloween fun

It's time for the annual fun night for children, when even the little ones are allowed to stay up late and call at neighbours' houses to play harmless tricks on them or accept small gifts of goodies. It's a night when neighbours can get to know one another.

'Trick or treat' becomes more popular every year and shops stock ever more exciting costumes and masks as well as bags of goodies for everyone. Everyone can enjoy the amazing outfits of witches, skeletons, ghosts and ghouls and even robots and monsters. Everyone can have a feast.

Halloween livens up the dark days of late autumn.

② Dangerous tricks and unhealthy treats

Tonight thousands of children are planning to go around bullying old people into giving them money or sweets. Bullying? Yes. Any behaviour that makes someone feel threatened or scared is bullying. They may call it harmless fun. That's what many bullies say about their callous behaviour.

'Trick or treat' is not an old tradition to keep up, but a modern import from the USA. It encourages children to misbehave with their identities disguised, to dress up specially to scare old people and to forget all they know about good behaviour.

They go around after dark, facing possible danger from traffic, and blackmail folk into giving them treats which they would be better off without: sackfuls of sickly chocolate and sweets oozing with tooth-rotting sugar.

There are many good reasons for banning this sinister practice.

Teachers' note The children should be able to identify immediately whether the writers approve or disapprove of 'trick or treat' on Halloween. In pairs, they could reread the reports and underline the parts that indicate bias, identifying and comparing the facts. Look for similarities but note that some facts are ignored and others are emphasised for effect.

A Lesson for Every Day
Literacy
9–10 Years
© A&C Black

LIVERPOOL JOHN MOORES UNIVERSITY
LEARNING SERVICES

A different bias: 2

- **Compare the two reports about Halloween.**
- **How can you tell that the writers are** $\boxed{\text{biased}}$ **?**
- **List the evidence.**

Report 1

Writer's point of view: _____

Examples of bias:

Adjectives _____

Nouns _____

Verbs _____

Opinions stated _____

as facts _____

Report 2

Writer's point of view: _____

Examples of bias:

Adjectives _____

Nouns _____

Verbs _____

Opinions stated _____

as facts _____

NOW TRY THIS!

- **Write an unbiased report about Halloween.**

Teachers' note Ask the children to reread the two reports on 'A different bias: 1' and to look for examples of language that present the facts in ways that express different opinions. Remind them of what they have learned about the connotations of words and point out how words can be used to appeal to a reader's emotions.

A Lesson for Every Day
Literacy
9–10 Years
© A&C Black

Dear Editor: 1

• Read these letters to a local newspaper.

1

Dear Editor

Summerton was a lovely village but over the years traffic has increased so much that the High Street is part of a major trunk road.

Huge lorries thunder through, shaking the very foundations of the old Tudor buildings and covering them with layers of oily dust. They pour out polluting gases that fill our lungs.

A bypass might take small slices off a few fields but the gain to the village will be immeasurable.

Yours faithfully

Anita Place, High Street

2

Dear Editor

Snobbs, the only department store in town, has big signs on its doors: "No unaccompanied children". This is an example of discrimination. It suggests that children are thieves, vandals or trouble-makers. Reading the columns of your newspapers, I find that more than 90% of the crimes in this town are committed by adults. It would be fairer if Snobbs' signs read "No unaccompanied adults".

I urge other children and young people to write to Snobbs to complain.

Yours faithfully

June O'Hoo (age 10), Market Street

3

Dear Editor

Our region offers perfect locations for wind turbines: open moorland at altitudes of up to 700 metres, largely uninhabited. Yet there are always strong objections to wind turbines. The objectors say they will spoil the landscape, create noise and damage wildlife. Would they prefer a silent but deadly form of damage in the form of nuclear power stations? That is what we will face if the country cannot generate enough electricity from renewables such as wind power.

Does anyone ever object to living close to a traditional windmill? I do not think so. We cannot go back in time. We have to build efficient, modern wind turbines.

Wind farms have their own beauty in the right setting. Nuclear power stations are always ugly.

Think about it before you protest.

Yours faithfully,

Lester Gripe, Top Heath

4

Dear Editor

I used to play football in the park but now I am not allowed to for two main reasons: children have been attacked and robbed there and the grass is fouled by dogs.

We all pay tax to the council. We deserve better than this. We need someone to supervise the park all the time it is open. This would keep park users safe. It would also help to stop vandalism and therefore save the council money. It would also help to catch dog-owners who do not clean up after their pets. They could enforce fines and this, too, would bring in money for the council. So the cost of employing a park supervisor would probably be more than paid for by the savings on repairs and the money from fines.

It makes no sense not to employ a supervisor.

Yours faithfully

Justin Goal (age 9), Match Green

Teachers' note After the children have read the letters, ask them about their purpose. Do they inform, ask for something, ask for information, explain, thank, congratulate or persuade? Ask the children how they can tell that these were written to persuade: focus on persuasive language, appeals to people's values and emotions, suggestions that any other view would be wrong and so on.

A Lesson for Every Day
Literacy
9-10 Years
© A&C Black

Dear Editor: 2

- **How do the letter-writers** persuade **their audience?**
- **Give examples.**

Persuasive technique	Letter	Examples
Presenting the facts in a biased way		
Sequencing the main points		
Comparison — What is compared with what?		
Presenting opinions as if they are facts		
Appealing to common sense		
Appealing to audience — Who are the audience? What might they value?		

Teachers' note Ask the children to reread the letters on 'Dear editor: 1' and to look for examples of persuasive language: bias, sequencing, comparisons, opinions given as facts, appeals to 'common sense' as if there is only one sensible view and appeals to the audience's known values.

A Lesson for Every Day
Literacy
9–10 Years
© A&C Black

Persuasive language

- **Look for examples of** [persuasive] **language.**
- **List them on the chart.**

Silver wheels

Probably the world's fastest heelies.

Do you want to impress your friends?

Here's your chance.

Take up our amazing offer.

Come and try a pair **FREE**.

Surely there could be no better offer.

Naturally, you'll find cheaper heelies but common sense will tell you that you only get what you pay for. If you want the best you'll want to pay that little bit more for what must be the perfect heelies.

- Specially designed by a top scientist so that there's almost **no friction**.
- Friction is what slows you down. Remove the friction and you'll move closer to the **speed of light**.
- The less friction the **faster** you go.

Powerful verbs	
Powerful adjectives	
Persuasive connectives	
Rhetorical questions	
Ambiguity	
Half-truths	

NOW TRY THIS!

- **Rewrite the text without any persuasive language.**

Just write the facts.

Teachers' note The children should read the advertisement and identify how the writer tries to influence the audience. They could underline the key words and phrases. Ask them to notice how this advertisement implies ideas without actually stating false facts.

Professor Phake's lecture

Professor Phake is persuading her audience that there are people living on Mars.

- **Put the points she makes into a logical order to write her lecture.**
- Link **them with** persuasive **words and phrases.**

Professor Phake's persuasion

Scientists used to say there could be no life on Mars because there was no water. Now they admit that there is some water.	These perfect domes could not have been created naturally,
The photographs have never been shown in the news in case they scared people.	When people laugh at the idea of life on Mars, just remember the proof you have seen.
The fact that there are roads shows that there are intelligent beings.	The fact that no one has seen Martians does not mean that they do not exist.
A lot of information about Mars has been kept secret. I am going to tell you those secrets.	There really is life on Mars. I am about to give you some proof.
Look at these lines along the ground. If we zoom in we can see that they are roads – on Mars!	We have photographs from the last Mars exploration that show domed buildings.

Persuasive expressions

clearly

every rational person

just think for a moment

it stands to reason

it would be madness

naturally

no one could doubt

surely

the most compelling evidence

there is no doubt

why should

without a doubt

you might wonder … but

Professor Phake's lecture

_____

_____

_____

_____

_____

_____

_____

_____

_____

_____

Teachers' note Here the children pretend to be Professor Phake trying to convince people that there is life on Mars. They should think of an introduction stating what the lecture is about and indicating her point of view, then support this with arguments and sum up in a way that reinforces the opening statement. It may help some children if they cut out and order the sentences before writing.

A Lesson for Every Day
Literacy
9-10 Years
© A&C Black

The persuader

Target job _____

- **Persuade a company to let you work for them for a day.**
- **Make** `notes` **on the chart.**
- **Cut out the notes and put them in the best order.**
- **Use them to help you to write a letter.**

Think about your useful knowledge, skills and personal qualities.

Dear Sir or Madam

I would like to come and work for your company for a day as a _____

I am certain that _____

_____

_____

_____

In addition to this _____

_____

_____

_____

You might think I am rather young for this work but _____

_____

_____

_____

_____

Yours faithfully _____

Teachers' note Ask the children to note down all the assets they think make them ideal for a particular job; also any points to counter any negative responses (for example 'too young', 'would hinder others', 'health and safety risk'). Each point should be in a separate box. They can then number the points or cut them out and put them in a logical order before writing.

A Lesson for Every Day
Literacy
9-10 Years
© A&C Black

Pigeons: 1

- **Read the** facts **about pigeons.**
- **Decide what a town council should do about the thousands of pigeons that roost on buildings in the town centre.**

Discuss this with your group.

The facts

Large numbers of pigeons in towns spread diseases, including lung disease.

Pigeon droppings and nests encourage insects such as beetles and moths.

Some people enjoy feeding and taming wild pigeons.

Some people in towns enjoy watching pigeons.

Some home-owners and business people do not like pigeon mess on their buildings.

If there is no food for pigeons they go somewhere else.

Pigeons can be scared by models of large birds (such as owls) and by electronic sounds.

Handlers of birds of prey, such as falcons, can be hired to let loose their birds to catch pigeons.

Pigeons in towns feed mainly on food waste from uncovered bins, as well as on the food people give them.

Sharp spikes or coils of wire fixed along gutters and ledges and around chimney pots stop birds landing and roosting there.

A sticky gel spread on surfaces stops pigeons landing there. They do not like the sticky feel.

It can cost about £2,000 per year to clean up pigeon mess in a town centre.

There are special cleaning materials to clean pigeon mess off stone and metal.

Animal-lovers do not like to see any birds harmed.

People cannot sit on benches in the town centre because of the pigeon mess on them.

Pigeon droppings leave pavements very slippery.

NOW TRY THIS!

- **List the** main points **you would make in a talk about pigeons in the town.**
- **Make** notes **about how you could present it to an audience.**

184

Teachers' note Tell the children that they are going to plan a talk on what should be done about large numbers of pigeons in a town centre. They should choose the facts that will support their argument. Different children or groups could present different solutions in order to open a class debate, ending with a vote. Use this with 'Pigeons: 2', which provides a structure to help the children to plan their talk.

A Lesson for Every Day
Literacy
9–10 Years
© A&C Black

Pigeons: 2

- **Write a** `talk` **to say what should be done about pigeons in the town centre.**

The town centre is full of pigeons. _____

_____

_____

> Say whether you welcome pigeons in the town centre.

> Explain why.

All sensible people will agree that _____

_____

_____

> Say what should be done.

If these actions are taken _____

_____

_____

> Say what the effects would be, and why.

There may be some who _____

_____

_____

> Mention other opinion and say why they are wrong.

The main issue is _____

_____

Surely _____

NOW TRY THIS!

- **Reread your talk.**
- **Add** `bullet points` **to help you to make your points when you present it to an audience.**

Teachers' note The children should first have completed 'Pigeons: 1'. Point out what the introduction is for (to state the purpose of the talk) and remind them to present the facts supporting their opinion in a way that persuades others to agree, through using persuasive language. Encourage them to mark the text to help when they read the talk: for example, with bullet points, or underlining words to stress.

A Lesson for Every Day
Literacy
9–10 Years
© A&C Black

Sacks of sentences

- **Sort the sentences below.**
- **Write the numbers in the sacks.**

Examples:

I like sprouts.

Statements

Do you like sprouts?

Questions

Please take the sprouts away.

Commands

I hate sprouts!

Exclamations

1 The weather is dreadful today.

2 Help me!

3 What is the weather like today?

4 How lovely!

5 We were lucky enough to see two otters in the river.

6 See if you can spot a water vole.

7 What's a water vole like?

8 It's like a brown rat but its tail is hairy, its ears are smaller and its nose isn't pointed.

9 Eeek – a rat!

10 They have been called water rats – wrongly.

NOW TRY THIS!

- **Write a new sentence about these for each sack:**

  spiders

  a river

Teachers' note Remind the children that some sentences are statements (they give information). Ask them about other types: questions ask something, commands or instructions tell the reader what to do and exclamations show emotions such as surprise, excitement, humour or shock. Read the first example with the children and discuss how to tell what kind of sentence it is.

A Lesson for Every Day
Literacy
9–10 Years
© A&C Black

Persuaders

Some words and phrases help to make a sentence ⟨persuasive⟩.

- Add a ⟨persuasive⟩ word or phrase to each sentence.

1 This is _____ the best thing to do.

2 _____ you agree with me.

3 He is _____ guilty.

4 _____ no-one would want to do that.

5 _____ we must stop the council closing the park.

6 These members must _____ want to stop the non-members coming in.

7 That is the best car, _____.

8 You will come to the fair, _____?

9 There is _____ nothing else we can do.

10 It would _____ be good for the town if we had a new supermarket.

11 The town _____ needs a bypass.

12 Children must be allowed in, _____?

Persuasion-bank

absolutely
certainly
clearly
definitely
don't you agree
don't you think
in any case
isn't it
naturally
obviously
of course
plainly
surely
without a doubt
you must

NOW TRY THIS!

- Write three persuasive sentences about a new shop which might open in the high street.

Teachers' note Read the first sentence with the children and then add a persuasive word, such as definitely in the gap. Ask them which sounds the more persuasive. They could try other words in the gap and decide which they think is the most effective.

A Lesson for Every Day
Literacy
9-10 Years
© A&C Black

187

Catchy ads

How have advertisers made these sentences appeal to their ⬚ audience ?
- **Write in the boxes:** ⬚ alliteration ⬚ rhyme ⬚ commands
- **Underline the alliterative words**
       rhyming words
       command sentences.

Some sentences use more than one of these.

Particular pooches prefer Doggy Diet. _____ _____	**Sale! Hurry! Only two days left.** _____ _____
Munchy Crunchy – the golden toffee treat. _____ _____	*Don't be slow – try Pro-Grow.* _____ _____
Reach for a peach. Pick your own fruit. _____ _____	**Stop! Drop into our drive-in deli.** _____ _____
Choose cheese – the munch for lunch. _____ _____	*Browse our best buys for a bargain.* _____ _____

NOW TRY THIS!

- **Write three advertising sentences for a theme park.**

Teachers' note Explain/remind the children of the meaning of alliteration and ask them for examples of rhymes and commands. Draw out that rhyme and alliteration help people to remember the advertisement and that command or instruction sentences help to persuade them.

A Lesson for Every Day
Literacy
9–10 Years
© **A&C Black**

Ghostly persuasion

The spook police have banned the ghosts from haunting places.
- **Use the** quotations **to help you to write an** argument **for the ghosts or the spook police.**

Ghosts have always haunted places. It is their right.

Ghosts have been able to haunt places for thousands of years but that doesn't mean they should do so for ever.

What if a ghost is just walking from one place to another? We could be accused of haunting when all we are doing is going for a walk!

Walking is fine but hanging around or loitering in places will be regarded as haunting.

Some people enjoy meeting ghosts. We provide a valuable service.

Many people are scared of ghosts. Scaring people counts as bullying.

We need to educate people so that they understand that ghosts won't harm them. Then they won't be scared.

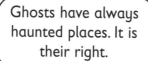

Introduction

_____

_____

State your opinion.

Arguments

_____

_____

_____

_____

_____

_____

Give reasons. Support your opinion. Say why it is right.

Conclusion

So _____

Repeat your opinion.

Teachers' note Copy this page onto A3 paper so that the children have plenty of space to write their argument. Remind them of useful persuasive words, phrases and clauses and how to use rhetorical questions (see notes on the activity on page 23).

A Lesson for Every Day
Literacy
9–10 Years
© A&C Black

189

Robert Louis Stevenson

- Read the poems aloud with a friend.
- Underline the parts you like the best.
- Write notes in the margins about why you like them.
- Link these to the correct line in the poem.

Block city

What are you able to build with your blocks?
Castles and palaces, temples and docks.
Rain may keep raining, and others go roam,
But I can be happy and building at home.

Let the sofa be mountains, the carpet be sea,
There I'll establish a city for me:
A kirk and a mill and a palace beside,
And a harbour as well where my vessels may ride.

Great is the palace with pillar and wall,
A sort of a tower on the top of it all,
And steps coming down in an orderly way
To where my toy vessels lie safe in the bay.

This one is sailing and that one is moored:
Hark to the song of the sailors aboard!
And see, on the steps of my palace, the kings
Coming and going with presents and things!

Now I have done with it, down let it go!
All in a moment the town is laid low.
Block upon block lying scattered and free,
What is there left of my town by the sea?

Yet as I saw it, I see it again,
The kirk and the palace, the ships and the men,
And as long as I live and where'er I may be,
I'll always remember my town by the sea.

The land of counterpane*

When I was sick and lay a-bed,
I had two pillows at my head,
And all my toys beside me lay,
To keep me happy all the day.

And sometimes for an hour or so
I watched my leaden soldiers go,
With different uniforms and drills,
Among the bed-clothes, through the hills;

And sometimes sent my ships in fleets
All up and down among the sheets;
Or brought my trees and houses out,
And planted cities all about.

I was the giant great and still
That sits upon the pillow-hill,
And sees before him, dale and plain,
The pleasant land of counterpane.

* a bed cover

Teachers' note Give the children time to read and enjoy the poems. They should read them (or listen to them being read) aloud to become aware of their rhythm and rhyme pattern. Discuss from whose point of view the poems are written and ask whether this reveals anything about the poet.

A Lesson for Every Day
Literacy
9-10 Years
© A&C Black

Grace Nichols

- **Read the poems with a friend.**
- **Underline the parts you like the best.**
- **Write notes in the margins about why you like them.**
- **Link these to the correct line in the poem.**

Sea timeless song

Hurricane come
and hurricane go
but sea... sea timeless

sea timeless
sea timeless
sea timeless
sea timeless

Hibiscus bloom
then dry-wither so
but sea... sea timeless

sea timeless
sea timeless
sea timeless
sea timeless

Tourist come
and tourist go
but sea... sea timeless

sea timeless
sea timeless
sea timeless
sea timeless

Early country village morning

Cocks crowing
Hens knowing
later they will cluck
their laying song

Houses stirring
a donkey clip-clopping
the first market bus
comes juggling along

Soon the sun will give a big yawn
and open her eye
pushing the last bit of darkness
out of the sky

NOW TRY THIS!

- **Compare these with the two poems by Robert Louis Stevenson.**

Think about the subject, theme, form, rhyme pattern and rhythm.

Teachers' note The children should read the poems (or listen to them being read) aloud to help become aware of the rhythm. Ask them how the poet uses language to create the image and feel of a real scene: for example, powerful verbs, nouns chosen for impact, personification and repetition, but no regular rhyme pattern.

Researching a poet

Poet's name ——————

Year of birth —————— Nationality ——————

Poem	Subject	Themes	Rhyme pattern	Language features: alliteration, simile, metaphor, comparison	Rhythm and pace

NOW TRY THIS!

• What do the poems tell you about the poet's background, interests and views?

• Write a report about the poet.

Teachers' note The children could begin by researching Robert Louis Stevenson and Grace Nichols. Ask them what they can infer from the poems about each writer. What do the scenes they describe and the words they use tell us about the writers – for example, their culture, aspects of their lives, their interests or way of looking at the world.

A Lesson for Every Day
Literacy
9-10 Years
© A&C Black

Free verse: 1

- ## Read the poem aloud with a friend.
- ## Draw the scenes it makes you imagine.

Taking my pen for a walk

Tonight I took the leash off my pen.
At first it was frightened,
looked up at me with confused eyes, tongue panting.
Then I said, "Go on, run away,"
and pushed its head.
Still it wasn't sure what I wanted;
it whimpered with its tail between its legs
So I yelled, "You're free, why don't you run –
you stupid pen, you should be glad,
now get out of my sight."
It took a few steps.
I stamped my foot and threw a stone.
Suddenly, it realised what I was saying
and began to run furiously away from me.

Julie O'Callaghan

Think about how to show the metaphor.

1	
2	**3**
4	**5**

eachers' note Ask the children if this is a prose passage or a poem. How they can tell? Then give
hem a copy of the page and ask them if they can tell more easily now. Ask how it is like prose and
raw out that it tells a story. Invite the children to describe the scenes each part makes them imagine.

A Lesson for Every Day
Literacy
9–10 Years
© A&C Black

193

Free verse: 2

- **Use your drawings to help you to write the story of the poem.**

Do not look at the poem. Cover it up. Use your own words.

_____

_____

_____

_____

_____

_____

_____

_____

_____

_____

_____

- **Read your story aloud.**
- **Listen to your group's stories.**
- **Compare them with the poem.**
- **What makes the poem poetic?**

Work in a group.

_____

Think about how the poem creates an image and how it makes you feel.

_____

_____

_____

_____

Think about how it does these.

_____

_____

Teachers' note Ask the children to reread the poem on 'Free verse: 1'. Ask how it makes them feel at different points. Cut out their numbered drawings from 'Free verse: 1' and use them to tell the story of the poem. Does this re-telling have the same effect? Why not? Draw out the effect of the powerful imagery through personification.

A Lesson for Every Day
Literacy
9–10 Years
© A&C Black

Build a poem

- **Work with a group.**
- **Build a house, village or town from construction materials.**
- **Imagine the place is real.**
- **What is it like there?**
- **Make** notes **to describe it.**
- **List useful** rhyming words .
- **Write a verse modelled on 'Block City'.**

> What are you able to build with your blocks?
> Castles and palaces, temples and docks.
> Rain may keep raining, and others go roam,
> But I can be happy and building at home.
>
> From 'Block City' by Robert Louis Stevenson

Notes

_____
_____
_____
_____
_____
_____
_____
_____
_____

Useful rhyming words

bricks	clicks, sticks, tricks
flower(s)	hour(s), our(s), power(s), shower(s)
lane	again, crane, drain, main, plain, rain, train

Our verse

Title _____

_____ (10 syllables)

_____ (10 syllables)

_____ (10 syllables)

_____ (10–11 syllables)

NOW TRY THIS!

- **Read your verse aloud.**
- **Check the** rhythm .

Does it make sense?

What are the mood and atmosphere like?

Does the rhyme pattern work?

Teachers' note Provide construction materials such as recycled materials or kits such as Lego and ask the children to make a model town or city. They could work in groups and discuss the structures they make and what the town or village is like, its surroundings, views, industry, other work and people. Then they can make notes to help them to write a verse modelled on the example from 'Block City'.

A Lesson for Every Day
Literacy
9–10 Years
© A&C Black

Early morning

- **Where do you think Grace Nichols' country village might be?**

  _____

- **How can you tell?**

  _____

  _____

  _____

- **Underline the** [free verse] **in the poem.**
- **Make** [notes] **about what you see and hear early in the morning in your locality.**
- **Write some ideas for personification.**
- **List some** [expressive words].

Early Country Village Morning

Cocks crowing
Hens knowing
later they will cluck
their laying song

Houses stirring
a donkey clip-clopping
the first market bus
comes juggling along

Soon the sun will give a big yawn
and open her eye
pushing the last bit of darkness
out of the sky

Grace Nichols

Notes	Personification and expressive words

NOW TRY THIS!

- **Write your own 'Early Morning' poem.**
- **Give it a** [title] **that describes the place.**

Teachers' note The children should first have read poems in which personification is used to create effects (see notes on the activity on page 24) and have discussed the ways in which it can intensify a feeling or atmosphere. To help them to come up with ideas, ask them to think about the effect they want (for example, speed, excitement, violence) and then imagine someone acting in these ways.

A Lesson for Every Day
Literacy
9–10 Years
© A&C Black

Free verse

- **What** metaphor **does the poet use for her pen?**

_____

- **Describe how it makes you** feel .

_____

_____

- **Write your own version of the poem. Make it happy, so the pen takes off and scribbles freely.**
- **Write in** free verse .

Tonight I took the leash off my pen.

Taking my Pen for a Walk

Tonight I took the leash off my pen.
At first it was frightened,
looked up at me with confused eyes, tongue panting.
Then I said, 'Go on, run away,'
and pushed its head.
Still it wasn't sure what I wanted;
it whimpered with its tail between its legs
So I yelled, 'You're free, why don't you run –
you stupid pen, you should be glad,
now get out of my sight.'
It took a few steps.
I stamped my foot and threw a stone.
Suddenly, it realised what I was saying
and began to run furiously away from me.

Julie O'Callaghan

_____
_____
_____
_____
_____
_____
_____
_____
_____
_____
_____
_____
_____
_____

You could say what the pen writes or draws.

You could describe any sounds the pen makes. (Keep to the metaphor.)

NOW TRY THIS!

- **Give your poem to a friend to read aloud.**
- **Listen carefully, then mark any parts you can improve.**

Teachers' note Read the poem with the children. Discuss its form and rhythm and ask them about any rhyme or other effects of sounds. Draw out that the poem does not follow any formal pattern, as it is in free verse. Ask how they would change it, still using the dog metaphor and in free verse, but making the pen seem happy to be given its freedom and with the poet expressing encouragement.

A Lesson for Every Day
Literacy
9–10 Years
© A&C Black

Soap opera challenge: 1

- ## Work in a group to plan and carry out this challenge.

Soap opera challenge

You are going to invent a new family of characters
for a soap opera. Your tasks are:

Task A – Plot
Write the plot outline of the first episode in which the family appears.

Task B – Setting
Write a description of the family's house and what it shows about the characters.

Task C – TV trailer
Plan and act out a TV trailer which introduces the family.

- ## Use the chart to plan what you will do. Discuss the questions on the notepad to help you.

How we will carry out the challenge

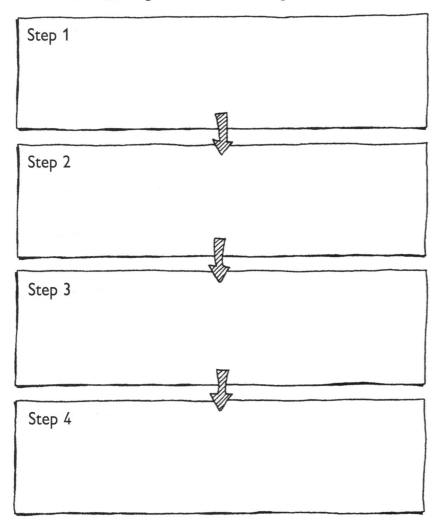

Step 1

Step 2

Step 3

Step 4

Questions

☆ What will the new characters be like?

☆ Who is the audience of the soap opera (children, adults or a mixture)?

☆ Who will do which tasks?

☆ How will everyone know what the others are doing?

☆ How long will the challenge take?

☆ How will we record our decisions?

☆ How will we present our work?

Teachers' note Use this with 'Soap opera challenge: 2 and 3'. Introduce the challenge (see notes on the activity on page 24), then split the class into groups of eight, so that pairs of children can carry out tasks A, B and C, and another pair can be 'directors' and oversee the whole group. (If there are smaller groups, they need not carry out all of the tasks.)

A Lesson for Every Day
Literacy
9-10 Years
© A&C Black

Soap opera challenge: 2

- Use this page to help you plan the new family of characters. You could use the pictures for ideas.

The _____ family

Character's name	Age	Appearance	Personality	Things he or she might say

- Now decide what hobbies or jobs your characters have. Think about how these will match their personalities.

Teachers' note Use this with 'Soap opera challenge: 1 and 3'. This sheet should be used once the children have completed the initial planning stage on 'Soap opera challenge: 1'. A chairperson should be appointed to make sure that everyone has their say and decisions are made as a group. One child should act as a scribe and record the group's ideas on the chart.

A Lesson for Every Day
Literacy
9–10 Years
© A&C Black

199

Soap opera challenge: 3

Task A – Plot

- **Plan the first episode in which the family appears. Draw your own flow chart and make notes on it.**

Beginning How will the episode start? Make it exciting.	**Middle** What will happen next?	**End** Make sure the audience will want to watch the next episode.

Task B – Plot

- **Make notes for your description of the family's house. You could also draw pictures.**

What kind of house will it be? Where will most of the action happen?

What will the children's bedrooms be like? Think about their hobbies.

Will the family have a garden? Will they have pets?

Task B – Plot

- **Make notes for your TV trailer which introduces the family. Then practise acting it out.**

How will you introduce the characters? Will you have a narrator?

What will the characters do and say?

How will you make the trailer exciting? Will you use sound effects?

Teachers' note Use this with 'Soap opera challenge: 1 and 2'. This sheet is intended to aid the children as they carry out tasks A, B and C of the challenge, outlined on 'Soap opera challenge: 1'. Each group will need one copy of the sheet; they should cut along the dotted lines and distribute the appropriate sections to the pairs carrying out each task.

A Lesson for Every Day Literacy 9–10 Years © A&C Black

How well did your group do?

My name _____

- **Fill in the chart.** Yes or No
- **Write an example in each line.**

For your teacher

Date _____

Activity _____

Talking and working together	Yes or No	Example
We planned a task.		
We carried out a task together that took a long time.		
We all had a chance to lead the group.		
We supported others in our group.		

What we could do better:

_____

_____

NOW TRY THIS!

- **Compare this with how you were at the start.**
- **What new skills do you have now?**

Teachers' note Use this to help the children to reflect on a discussion they had and to consider what they said and did that helped the discussion to achieve a target: planning a task, collecting information, carrying out and using a survey, carrying out a task over a long period (including checking progress and making any necessary changes), supporting others in the group.

A Lesson for Every Day
Literacy
9-10 Years
© **A&C Black**

201

Aladdin playscript

- **Work in a group. You are going to write a scene for the pantomime *Aladdin*.**
- **Read the cast list and the plot. Discuss what will happen in your scene. You do not have to use all the characters.**

The cast

Aladdin	A bright, honest peasant boy
Widow Twanky	A washerwoman; mother of Aladdin, Wishee and Washee
Wishee and Washee	Aladdin's younger twin brothers (not very bright)
Abanazer	An evil magician
Emperor	The Emperor of China
Princess So-Shi	The Emperor's beautiful daughter
Genie of the lamp	A magical genie who can grant any wish

The plot

The evil magician Abanazer hears of a magic lamp hidden in a cave in China. He travels there and looks for a peasant boy who will fetch the lamp for him. Aladin is working in his mother's laundry when Abanazer arrives and pretends to be his long-lost uncle. Aladdin goes to the cave and finds the lamp, but decides not to give it to Abanazer. When he refuses to hand it over, Abanazer magically locks him in the cave. Wondering how he will escape, Aladdin rubs the lamp. To his amazement, a Genie appears and grants him any wish. Aladdin not only escapes, but becomes the richest person in China! Aladdin asks to marry the beautiful princess and she accepts. However, evil Abanazer kidnaps the princess, steals the lamp and runs off to Egypt. Aladdin and his friends follow on a magic carpet and defeat Abanazer once and for all. Aladdin and the princess are married, and the Emperor falls for Widow Twanky!

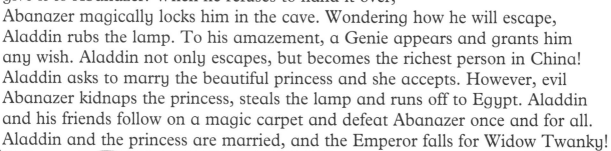

- **Write your scene. Use the features of pantomime.**
- **You need the sheets called *Aladdin characters* and *Model theatre*. Make the characterss and the theatre.**

NOW TRY THIS!

- **Perform your scene to the rest of the class.**
- **Discuss how successful your performance was. Did you audience react in the way you expected?**

202

Teachers' note Split the class into groups of four to six and give each group one copy of this page and of 'Aladdin characters' and 'Model theatre'. First revise the features of pantomime (see page 44) and how to write a playscript. Read the cast list and the plot together, and explain to the children that they are going to write a scene for performance in a model theatre.

A Lesson for Every Day
Literacy
9–10 Years
© A&C Black

Aladdin characters

Colour and cut out the characters.
Tape each charater
to a drinking straw.
Use the characters
in your model theatre.

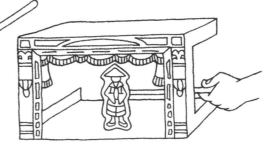

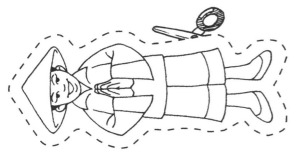
Washee

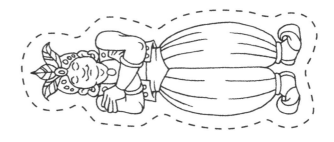
Genie

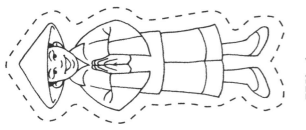
Wishee

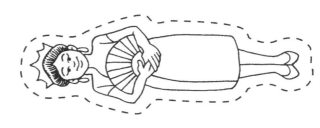
Princess So-Shi

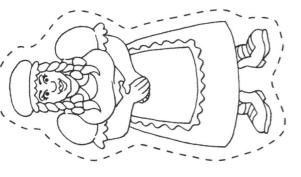
Widow Twanky

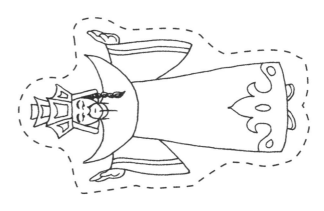
Emperor

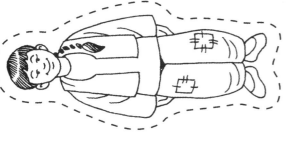
Aladdin

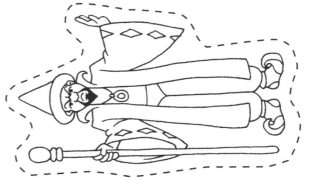
Abanazer

Teachers' note Use this with 'Aladdin playscript' and 'Model theatre'. Photocopy this page onto card if possible. Each group will need eight drinking straws, scissors, coloured pencils and sticky tape. The characters can be used in the model theatre by inserting them through the holes in the sides.

A Lesson for Every Day
Literacy
9–10 Years
© A&C Black

Model theatre

Teachers' note Use this with 'Aladdin playscript' and 'Aladdin characters'. You will need to demonstrate how to make the model. The children could make additional scenery and props.

A Lesson for Every Day
Literacy
9–10 Years
© A&C Black

Weird words

- **Read the description then find the weird word.**
- **Write the word in the box.**

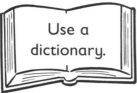
Use a dictionary.

My weird word begins with a consonant, followed by an unstressed vowel. It ends with a segment that sounds like `shum`.

My weird word begins with a soft `c`. The middle vowel is unstressed. It ends with a vowel.

My weird word has the phoneme `oo` followed by a short `o` phoneme that is part of the suffix `ology`, but there is an `o` missing.

My weird word has two `k` phonemes and two phonemes that are written `u`. It ends with the unstressed vowel phoneme `er`.

My weird word begins with a `z` phoneme written `x`, then the phoneme `igh` written `y`. It ends with the suffix `phone` (sound).

It is a compound word, has a double consonant in the middle and ends with the letters `ing`, which are not a suffix here.

My weird word has the suffix `ary` after an unstressed vowel and a consonant.

My weird word has the suffix `ment` after an unstressed vowel and a consonant that is difficult to hear.

My weird word has an unstressed vowel followed by an `n` phoneme spelt `gn`.

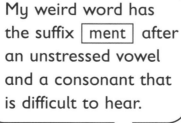
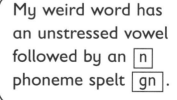

eachers' note Point out that one way of learning how to spell a difficult or irregular word is to look at closely and describe its main features. The children could practise this for one new word each week. heir words and descriptions could be displayed for others to match up.

A Lesson for Every Day
Literacy
9–10 Years
© A&C Black

205

Words of a feather

- Write a word on each wing whose meaning is linked to the word in the bird's beak.
- Use the underlined segment.

Use a dictionary.

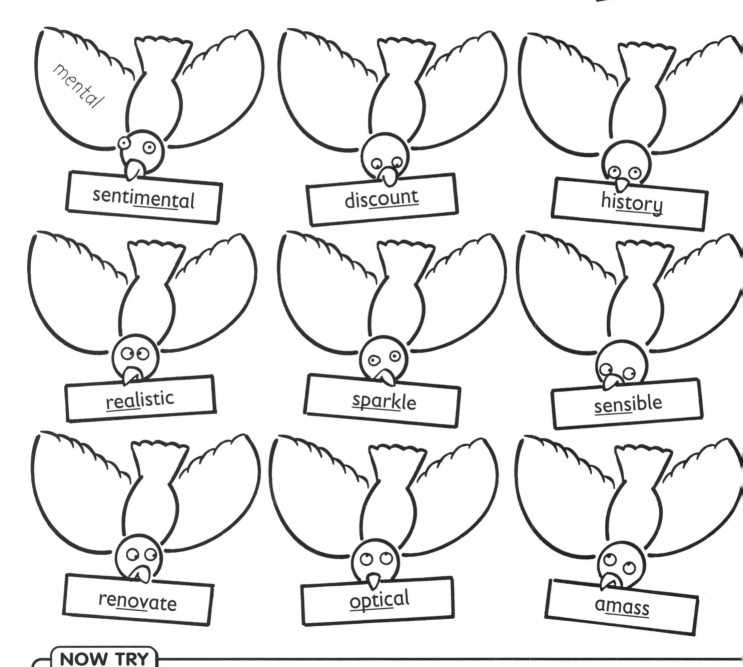

mental

sentimental

discount

history

realistic

sparkle

sensible

renovate

optical

amass

NOW TRY THIS!

- Choose a bird.
- Write sentences using each of the words.

The sentences should show the meanings of the words.

206

Teachers' note Use the first example to help them to get started: where possible, they should try to find one entire word within the word shown (for example, mental). If they can think of more than two words for any example, they could write it on the bird's body.

A Lesson for Every Day
Literacy
9–10 Years
© A&C Black

Is there anybody there?

Teachers' note Use this activity to introduce the classic narrative poem *The Listeners* by Walter de la Mare ('The listeners'). Explore the setting. What can they see? What time of the day is it? What might they hear in this setting and what might it fell like to step into it? Ask them what might happen there. Who might come into the setting, and from where?

The traveller

Teachers' note The children should first have carried out the activity on 'Is anybody there?'. Now introduce the central character in the poem (see also 'The listeners'). Remind the children of the setting and ask them who this might be. Why is he knocking on the door? Introduce some language used in the poem to describe the arrival of the traveller.

A Lesson for Every Day
Literacy
9–10 Years
© A&C Black

'The Listeners'

- **Underline the words that are important in creating the atmosphere of the poem.**
- **On the side write notes about the** | atmosphere |.
- **Act the scene with a friend.**

> Look for features such as rhyme, alliteration, onomatopoeia and lengths of lines.

The Listeners

"Is there anybody there?" said the Traveller,
   Knocking on the moonlit door;
And his horse in the silence champed the grasses
   Of the forest's ferny floor:
And a bird flew up out of the turret,
   Above the Traveller's head:
And he smote upon the door a second time;
   "Is there anybody there?" he said.
But no one descended to the Traveller;
   No head from the leaf-fringed sill
Leaned over and looked into his grey eyes,
   Where he stood perplexed and still.
But only a host of phantom listeners
   That dwelt in the lone house then
Stood listening in the quiet of the moonlight
   To that voice from the world of men:
Stood thronging the faint moonbeams on the dark stair,
   That goes down to the empty hall,
Hearkening in an air stirred and shaken
   By the lonely Traveller's call.
And he felt in his heart their strangeness,
   Their stillness answering his cry,
While his horse moved, cropping the dark turf,
   'Neath the starred and leafy sky;
For he suddenly smote on the door, even
   Louder, and lifted his head –
"Tell them I came, and no one answered,
   That I kept my word," he said.
Never the least stir made the listeners,
   Though every word he spake
Fell echoing through the shadowiness of the still house
   From the one man left awake:
Ay, they heard his foot upon the stirrup,
   And the sound of iron on stone,
And how the silence surged softly backward,
   When the plunging hoofs were gone.

Walter de la Mare

Teachers' note You could provide a 'story bag' containing objects for the children to explore before they read the poem (see notes on the activity on page 25). They could read it for themselves, to enjoy it, before you read it aloud with them to explore the use of language.

A Lesson for Every Day
Literacy
9–10 Years
© A&C Black

209

'The Listeners' atmosphere

Read *The Listeners* **on page 209.**

- **Which of these cards describe the poem's atmosphere best?**

blustery	calm	dismal
echoing	eerie	foreboding
ghostly	grim	haunted
hushed	light-hearted	menacing
noiseless	mysterious	peaceful
quiet	romantic	silent
sinister	soundless	still
threatening	tranquil	uneasy

Teachers' note The children should first have carried out the activity on 'Is there anybody there?', 'The traveller' and 'The listeners'. Ask the children to sort the cards according to how well they describe the atmosphere of the poem. Ask them to look for evidence in the poem to support their choices.

A Lesson for Every Day
Literacy
9-10 Years
© A&C Black

Listening to poems

- Use this page to record your responses to poems you listen to.

Title	Poet	Rythym – and changes	Pace – and changes	Mood – and changes	Message or meaning

NOW TRY THIS!

- Write your ideas about what makes a poem good to read aloud.

Teachers' note Ask the children what difference it makes to hear a poem rather than read it to themselves. Focus on the way in which this can bring out rhyme, rhythm and other features that help to communicate meaning.

A Lesson for Every Day
Literacy
9–10 Years
© A&C Black

211

Read it aloud

- **Plan how to read the poem aloud.**
- **Practise with a friend.**

Each verse should be read differently. Think about tone of voice.

I shall – so there!

Just you wait!

Warning

When I am an old woman I shall wear purple
With a red hat which doesn't go, and doesn't suit me,
And I shall spend my pension on brandy and summer gloves
And satin sandals, and say we've no money for butter.
I shall sit down on the pavement when I'm tired
And gobble up samples in shops and press alarm bells
And run my stick along the public railings
And make up for the sobriety of my youth.
I shall go out in my slippers in the rain
And pick the flowers in other people's gardens
And learn to spit.

I'll do as I like!

Ha! Ha!

You can wear terrible shirts and grow more fat
And eat three pounds of sausages at a go
Or only bread and pickle for a week
And hoard pens and pencils and beermats and things in boxes.

But now we must have clothes that keep us dry
And pay our rent and not swear in the street
And set a good example for the children.
We will have friends to dinner and read the papers.

Very nice.

But maybe I ought to practise a little now?
So people who know me are not too shocked and surprised
When suddenly I am old and start to wear purple.

Jenny Joseph

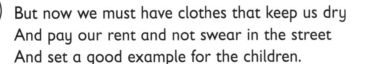
Tut, tut! Fancy doing that.

NOW TRY THIS!

- **Describe the changes from one verse to another.**

Teachers' note Use this page to help the children to read a poem aloud in a way that brings out its humour. Point out the title and ask who is warning whom. What is she warning about? Discuss different warning tones: for example, threatening or menacing, light-hearted and 'just watch me'.

A Lesson for Every Day
Literacy
9-10 Years
© A&C Black

Sounds good

- **Read the poem aloud.**
- **What makes it sound good?**
- **Underline the effective words.**
- **Write notes about what makes these parts sound good.**
- **Link them to the right place in the poem.**

Leisure

What is this life if, full of care,
We have no time to stand and stare.

No time to stand beneath the boughs
And stare as long as sheep or cows.

No time to see, when woods we pass,
Where squirrels hide their nuts in grass.

No time to see, in broad daylight,
Streams full of stars like skies at night.

No time to turn at Beauty's glance,
And watch her feet, how they can dance.

No time to wait till her mouth can
Enrich that smile her eyes began.

A poor life this if, full of care,
We have no time to stand and stare.

W H Davies

NOW TRY THIS!

- **What is the message of this poem?**
- **Describe how the poet's choice of words helps to communicate this message.**

Teachers' note Let the children read this poem to themselves and give them time to respond to it before asking them about its message and meaning, atmosphere and mood and the words and phrases that communicate these. Ask them how they think it should be read.

A Lesson for Every Day
Literacy
9–10 Years
© A&C Black

213

Sounds good to me

- **What are your favourite poems to listen to?**
- **Write the lines you like to hear.**
- **Note what you like about them.**

Think about the effects of…
rhythm, rhyme, alliteration,
onomatopoeia, powerful verbs
and adjectives.

Title	Poet	Line	What I like about the sound

NOW TRY THIS!

- **Describe the effects of these lines of poetry.**

Teachers' note After listening to several poems read aloud, the children could choose their four favourites to listen to. Ask them to think about what makes them good to listen to, particularly how effects such as rhyme and rhythm help to communicate meaning and atmosphere.

A Lesson for Every Day
Literacy
9–10 Years
© A&C Black

Performance evaluator

- **Evaluate a** `performance` **of a poem.**
- **How well did the performance bring out:**

| the mood of the poem: humorous, sad, exciting, mysterious? | the meaning of the poem? | changes in atmosphere? | build-up of tension, story, character, mystery? |

Poem _____ by _____

Points to think about	How they were used	Effects
Volume (loud voices, quiet voices, changes in volume)		
Pace (fast, slow, changes in pace)		
Expression (using voices to express feelings, mood, atmosphere)		
Facial expressions		
Movement		
Other (for example, sound effects, props, costume, masks)		

NOW TRY THIS!

- **Write one suggestion that would improve this performance.**
- **Explain how it would help.**

eachers' note The children can use this page to help them to identify the criteria by which to judge
he performance of a poem. They can also use these criteria to help them to plan a performance.
.sk them to experiment with their voices, facial expressions and movements in order to find the most
.ffective.

A Lesson for Every Day
Literacy
9–10 Years
© A&C Black

215

Performance poet

- **Plan your own** `performance poem` **using 'Adventures of Isabel' as a model.**
- **Make up a new character. Instead of meeting other characters he or she could go to dangerous or exciting places.**
- **Think about what the character might do or collect there.**

Character	Places visited
Name	
Description	
Amusing or interesting characteristics Fearless? Clumsy? Funny? Forgetful? Vain? Other?	What the character does or collects there Food? Gadgets? Pets? Other things?

Poem plan

Number of verses Number of lines per verse Repetition and examples Vowels? Consonants? Words? Phrases?	Rhyme pattern and examples Couplets? Alternate lines? Every fourth line? Other?
Ideas for chorus	Rhythm

NOW TRY THIS!

- **Write the first verse of your poem.**
- **Read it aloud with a friend and** `edit` **it.**
- **Use this to help you to write the second verse.**

Teachers' note The children will need a copy of the poem 'Adventures of Isabel' by Ogden Nash. Ask them to think up their own character and to write descriptive notes about him or her, including personal qualities: Isabel was fearless but the new character might be forgetful, vain or clumsy. Then they can imagine places this character goes and what happens there.

A Lesson for Every Day
Literacy
9–10 Years
© A&C Black